Sales Management
Power Strategies

Building a replicable and scalable sales process

Paul R. DiModica

Publisher's Note

This book is designed to provide accurate and authoritative information in regard to the subject matter covered. It is sold with the understanding that neither the author nor the publisher is engaged in rendering legal, accounting, or other professional service. If legal advice or other expert assistance is required, the services of a competent professional person should be sought.

Copyright © 2006 Paul R. DiModica All rights reserved.

No part of this publication or training course may be reproduced, recorded, redistributed, taught, stored in a retrieval system, or transmitted, in any form or by any means, electronic, mechanical, photocopying, recording, or otherwise, without the prior written permission of the publisher.

First Edition.

International Standard Book Number: 1-933598-28-X

Published by Johnson & Hunter, Inc. (www.johnsonhunter.com)

Trademarks

All terms mentioned in this book that are known to be trademarks or service marks have been appropriately capitalized. Johnson & Hunter cannot attest to the accuracy of this information. Use of a term in this book should not be regarded as affecting the validity of any trademark or service mark.

Bulk Sales

Johnson & Hunter offers excellent discounts on this book when ordered in quantity for bulk purchases or special sales. For more information, please contact **corpsales@johnsonhunter.com**.

Cover

Image by Digital Vision/Getty Images

Dedication

In memory of my dad, John,
who inspired me to always try harder,
to be honest,
and to never say I can't do something—
while simultaneously reminding me
family always comes first.

Table of Contents

Preface ix

Chapter 1 The Complexities of Sales Management 1
   Sales Savants Need Not Apply 1
   Current State of the Market 2
   Turning Revenue Strategy into Action Steps—Alignment of Sales Management Goals 7
   Establishing a Solid Foundation for the Sales Team 10
   Understanding the Origins and Pillars of Integrated Pillar Management 15
   Understanding Executive Management Types and Their Effects On Sales Management 19

Chapter 2 Developing a Sales Process 33
   Evaluating Your Sales Strategy 37
   Developing a Replicable and Scaleable Sales Process 42
   Pulling It All Together and Documenting Your Sales Process 48

Chapter 3 Organizing the Structure of Your Sales Team 51
   Understanding Sales Personality Types 52
   Determining Your Company's Business Life Cycle 62
   Matching Business Life Cycle with Personality Types 65
   Types of Sales Team Positions 68
   Using the Pursuit Sales Team Model to Maximize Key Account Success 72
   Pursuit Sales Team Process Model 77

Chapter 4 Hiring the Right Salespeople 79
   Full-Cycle Salespeople versus Half-Cycle Salespeople ... 79
   Finding Good Salespeople 83
   Hiring Salespeople Based on Your Business Needs 84
   Evaluating Candidates 88
   The Hiring Tool That Makes or Breaks a Candidate 100
   Investing in Your Sales Team 102
   Managing Cultural Performance 104

Table of Contents

    Establishing Sales Job Descriptions 108
    Success Factors of Salespeople Who Hit Their Quota ... 113

Chapter 5 Sales Team Compensation Plans 115
    Developing a Compensation Plan 117
    Implementing New Sales Compensation Plans 120
    Developing an Incentive Program 121

Chapter 6 Training Salespeople 125
    6 Reasons Why Most Companies Do Not Give More Sales Training 126
    Guidelines for Training Your Sales Team 127
    Making Your Sales Training More Successful 128
    Role-Playing Tips to Increase Success 129

Chapter 7 Managing Your Sales Team 135
    Managing Salespeople Who Work in Virtual Offices 135
    Managing the Salesperson Ride-Along 137

Chapter 8 Holding Sales Meetings 143
    Holding Team Meetings 143
    Holding One-on-One Meetings 145
    Developing Weekly/Monthly Manager Action Plans 147
    Weekly Sales Activities Report 149
    Topics for Your Monthly Sales Meetings 151

Chapter 9 Determining Sales Quotas 153
    Common Quota Calculation Mistakes 153
    Calculating Sales Quotas 157
    Understanding Lost Sales Analysis 162
    Calculating Lost Sales Analysis & Sales Effectiveness . 165
    Resources for Market Research 169
    19 Factors That Affect a Salesperson's Performance 170

Chapter 10 Managing Forecasts 173
    Controlling "Sales Forecasting Moles" 173
    Creating a Sales Forecast 179
    Tightening the Sales Forecast 183
    Differentiating Between a Forecast and a Pipeline 184
    Sales Closing Audit 185

Table of Contents

Chapter 11 Managing Sales by Metrics 187
   Identifying Major Sales Metrics 187
   Evaluating Your Sales Team's Performance 193
   Sales Team Monthly Assessment 195

Chapter 12 Managing Strategic Alliances and Channel Partners 199
   Understanding Strategic Replication—Alliance Partner Collectives..199
   Strategic Partner Management—Rules to Guide Alliances and Collectives to Increase Sales......................................203

Chapter 13 Using Sales Scorecards to Manage More Effectively..209
   Understanding the Sales Scorecard Concept 213
   Preparing a Sales Scorecard..216
   Implementing the Sales Scorecard..................................220

Chapter 14 Integrated Pillar Management 223
   Integrating the Pillars..223
   6-Week Implementation Plan 235

Chapter 15 Teaching Ethics and Morality 241
   6 Guidelines on How to Communicate and Deploy Ethical Standards to Your Sales Team...243

Conclusion 247

Example Forms 251

Index 259

Table of Contents

Preface

Sales management can be described as "standing barefoot on a sharp samurai battle sword while juggling uncooked eggs over your head."

Managing the function of sales is not a simple process. It requires a full-time, dedicated, premeditated process that allows you to create replicable and scalable programs that you can maintain and expand.

Today, more than ever, business success is centered on sales and revenue capture. Product and service delivery, corporate customer care, and operation development are important; but, without sufficient revenues for your firm to grow, their need is minimal.

Through our value forward approach, we will help you develop powerful sales management techniques, strategies, and business processes to help manage your sales team more effectively and grow your business.

More than ever, the value of your business is not based on the product or service you sell but on the strength of your sales and marketing distribution.

Our value forward approach to sales management guides you through a premeditated

process to help you hire correctly and grow your business by training and managing your sales team to increase your sales success.

Chapter 1

The Complexities of Sales Management

After reading this chapter, you will know:

- Why organizational structures of the past are not beneficial to today's business operating models

- How integrating key departments will increase company performance

- How to establish a solid foundation for the sales department

- What characteristics are typically found in management executives and how those characteristics affect their management style

Sales Savants Need Not Apply

Today it is difficult to find good salespeople. They are out there—but more often than not, they are hidden in the back cubicles of your competitor's office.

Chapter 1
The Complexities of Sales Management

Where are the sales hunters who can make your sales team successful?[1]

Can you name all of the companies that were dominant players in your market in 1980?

Where are they today?

If they are still around, what sales model do they currently operate under?

If they failed, how much did they spend on expensive consulting companies that ultimately painted their paths to failure?

To be successful in sales management, you need to maximize the investment you have in your current sales team and set a pattern of team management that will help you and future sales team members become more successful.

Current State of the Market

The mechanics of sales management for many companies is currently stuck in a cyclic format that was developed before 1980: annual sales projections based on backroom conversations with unsubstantiated forecast logic, marketing departments that spend money rather than create qualified inbound lead generation for the sales team,

---
[1] For more information on this topic, see my book, *Value Forward Selling: How to Sell to Management* located at www.howtoselltomanagement.com.

and strategy managers who make judgmental observations on new product and service offerings independent of what salespeople can sell.

While many industries continue to evolve their operational capabilities around the Internet and the digital economy, many executives continue to manage their companies based on **antiquated management concepts** carried over from the organizational structures of Fortune 500 corporations or some business article they read in a trade publication for their industry. In doing so, they stagnate the growth of their firms as they attempt to grow revenue with aging sales management methodologies.

In this paradox, there are:

- VPs of Sales who are held accountable for annual sales forecasts that were created twelve months prior in industries where economic conditions change every six months

- VPs of Marketing who are not paid on revenue, but are provided bonuses based on marketing and communications (MARCOM) objectives

- VPs of Operations or customer care departments who approve sales proposals based on their department's fulfillment needs instead of what customers want to buy

Chapter 1
The Complexities of Sales Management

So, whose fault is this?

Well, it is not the fault of the vice president of sales, the vice president of marketing, or the vice president of operations. Like all of us have been from time to time, they are stuck in a traditional corporate organizational structure with silo decision-making that reduces the potential for integrated sales management processes. This organizational structure does not work well for growth-focused companies because growth-focused companies are innately different from traditional companies.

It is the question of how companies manage sales that needs to be examined.

When analyzing small business start-ups, mature family businesses, and Fortune 1000 players, we consistently see the same organizational structure and recurring compensation plans for sales management. At times, innovative sales management programs are in place, leading firms to accelerated growth; but for most companies, the basic process of managing a sales department has not changed since the early 1980s. There are vice president of sales, sales managers, and account executives following the same belief: sales management is all about helping your sales team get the contract or purchase order. They are right in one respect ... but sales management is *more* than that.

This antiquated sales management process exists throughout the entire world, in big companies and small, start-ups, and invisible corporations. Many times, their management structures are based on the bureaucracy of a Fortune 500 organizational chart that focuses on discipline and is **designed to create order, not sales revenue**.

Sales management is also about hiring and managing the right salespeople, tracking their performance by metrics during the sales cycle, and working with your management team to develop long-term planning and budgeting.

Yet, we are all willing participants in the traditional model of organizational structure, without necessarily realizing it. When an investor suggests a start-up founder hire an experienced president to run the day-to-day, whom does he recommend and approve? Most often, he selects an executive from a large competitor or a Fortune 1000 company, when he should be selecting someone with experience in starting and/or growing a young company.

When a $10 million CEO wants to hire a vice president of sales to double her company's revenue, whom does she hire? Usually, it is a regional vice president of sales from a $1 billion powerhouse, when it should be someone with experience in growing a company from $10 million to $50 million.

When a Fortune 500 company seeks a new divisional senior vice president of sales, whom does it select? Either a vice president from within the organization is promoted or a new vice president from a direct Fortune 500 competitor is brought in.

These are examples of how the Fortune 500 model is used as the foundation of most organizational structures, regardless of the size of the firm. Fortune 500 means just that – "we are one of the top 500 firms" not "we are trying to *grow* to be one of the top 500 firms." And for that reason, the Fortune 500 model does not always work well in start-up or growth-directed firms where aggressive expansion is needed, risky decisions are made, and unconventional methods are used to gain an edge.

We are cogs in the machine that is laid out before us. We just keep recycling the Fortune 500 structure from firm to firm. Each new executive brings with her an "established" way of sales management and continues the cycle, or a start-up founder reads in a business publication "the way" it is supposed to be and then emulates the corporate mentors he aspires to be like.

This happens because Fortune 500 sales management models need discipline and are based on non-shifting industries, rigid markets, and years of established business structure needed to manage pre-programmed budgets and operating markets. They have very detailed job descriptions, budgets, staff positions, line positions, sales forecasts, pay plans, and weekly executive meetings—all based on big companies' business needs to manage by department. However, this management structure often creates friction between the sales department and the other department heads that directly influence revenue generation. Instead of building a successful sales team environment, it builds permanent silos.

Turning Revenue Strategy into Action Steps—Alignment of Sales Management Goals

To grow your firm, your business competence will not be determined by the quality of the product or service you sell. Yes, they are important, but there are many case studies of companies with great customer offerings that failed because their sales process was inferior.

Conversely, there are many companies today with products or services that are not competitive and yet their revenues are growing dramatically because of their sales teams' management skills.

You notice, I didn't say sales *staff* skills.

Many times in sales-driven companies, singular successful salespeople become the figureheads or poster boys (or girls) as the prototype sales approach the company wants to duplicate. But individual sales success is oftentimes an anomaly that can't be repeated and aligning your sales management model around one person's success is not the way to grow your company.

Chapter 1
The Complexities of Sales Management

Yes, understanding the strategic and tactical techniques used by the top salesperson in your firm is important, but you must make sure these learned observations can be replicated for continued success and will help create a sales prototype model for the team as a whole.

Your goal as a sales manager is to develop a sales process that is scalable and replicable and can be documented, so you can forecast revenues to management with some accuracy. This approach helps sales management executives create a business environment where they can be held accountable for their department only.

Often, the sales manager is the first executive to be held accountable when department or company revenues are down.

But, is this fair?

- Why should the sales manager be held accountable if the marketing department cannot generate qualified leads?

- Why should the sales manager be held responsible because the strategy department incorrectly forecast a market gap size?

- Why should the sales manager be measured poorly if the strategic partner or channel manager generates no leads from existing alliances?

- Why should the sales manager be held accountable if the operations department produces red shoes when prospects want to buy blue shoes?

- Why should the sales manager be held accountable if the accounting or finance department non-competitively priced the company's products or services?

Today, the key to success is a premeditated, outbound sales development program that helps you, as a sales manager, become "visibly successful."

Firms need to focus a 360° integration of their company's departments to increase revenue. When one singular department fails to contribute, it directly affects all corporate revenue opportunities. At that point, it is not the sales department's failure to generate revenue; it is the company's failure.

This 360° approach of **modern** sales management includes the integration of five pillars:

1. Sales
2. Marketing
3. Strategy
4. Product Development/Operations
5. Strategic Partners/Alliances

In Chapter 14, I'll guide you through the integration of these five pillars and provide a 6-week implementation plan.

All of these departments contribute to the success or failure of a sales manager and his sales team. Sales management is not a silo, but rather a catalyst for revenue growth through the intersection of these five pillars. To succeed, these departments need to be positioned as a team to increase corporate revenue.

It is not the sales department's responsibility for revenue—it is the company's responsibility.

Establishing a Solid Foundation for the Sales Team

My discovery of the integrated sales management success factor using this approach arose out of necessity in 1986, when I was the District Sales Manager for a firm headquartered out of Toronto, Ontario. At the time, I was selling $50,000 to $150,000 Point of Sales (POS) hardware, software, and professional services to independent restaurant owners up and down the street in a regional territory. Restaurant owners (even today) do not like too much automation because it tracks the cash element of their businesses.

In 1986, it was almost unheard of for a restaurant owner to install a computer system.

Chapter 1
The Complexities of Sales Management

In those days, my sales team and I competed on a day-to-day basis against a major billion-dollar computer corporation that dominated the cash register/POS market space. At my company, we had a POS system that was the first CPU computer-based cash register system available. Prior to our product's introduction, all other cash register systems ran on intelligent registers that were ganged together in a communications loop.

Keep in mind, in 1986, a $100,000+ cash register system was like a $300,000 investment today—a lot of money for a family owned restaurant to spend then, as well as now.

Our POS system worked on an operating system, the CPM 86, which was manufactured by Digital Research, a firm based in California. It was truly advanced technology and allowed us to operate 30 (yes 30) dumb terminals attached to a PC running simultaneously on an 8086 chip that delivered orders to the kitchen and managed inventory, cash, and staffing all at the same time.

To complicate matters, the price of my firm's product was TWICE the cost of our billion-dollar competitor that owned the majority of the market share. From a pure **functionality** standpoint, our system was **only** 20% better than competing products, but it was **100% more money**!

Very early in my sales management career (out of necessity), I learned that to sell and hit my team's sales quota, I needed a more involved approach than a traditional sales management model to help my sales team succeed.

So in 1986, I wrote down these **five sales management steps** to help my team and I sell a $100,000 restaurant system from an unknown start-up that was twice the price of the existing market leader.

The five-step sales management structure includes:

1. Creating a successful sales strategy and sales process that can be documented and forecasted.

2. Understanding how to hire, motivate, and lead salespeople.

3. Developing a sales toolbox that allows me to measure my sales team members by business metrics, not emotion.

4. Creating a sales management environment that works as a liaison between senior management and the sales staff.

5. Partnering with other departments, including marketing, strategy, and operations, to align the success of the sales department with their help.

Chapter 1
The Complexities of Sales Management

Without knowing it, I had created today's modern business model for sales management.

That year, I sold approximately $1,500,000 of POS systems, service, software, training, and professional services; and all of my sales team members hit their individual sales quotas of $1,000,000, that included software, training, hardware, cabling, and maintenance (in 1986 dollars).

As a team, we had a total of 1% discount off the suggested retail price of all of the products and services we sold, even though our offerings were 100% more money than our Fortune 500 competition.

The key here is not what I did, but *how* I did it and what affect it had on my team's sales revenue once I became a sales manager.

From that day forward, I recognized I had started a unique sales management approach (for myself and any company I worked for) to be more successful. I observed early on that integrating the sales, strategy, sales management, and marketing tools at a company's disposal—a united program—could increase revenue for each individual, for the sales team as a group, and for the company as a whole.

Although this new sales management approach was born out of necessity—I wanted to keep my job—from the beginning it seemed to make sense and I found it to be different than how "other" sales managers approached their jobs.

It was not that other sales managers purposefully built barriers to work as sales managers in a silo process, but more that they acted this way in response to the ever-present pressure to generate more revenue immediately for their sales teams. **Nevertheless, working independently is the wrong thought process.**

Where are the 1980's companies that continued to think inside the box and were advised by big five consulting companies on traditional business sales models?

Where are the 1990's companies that focused on the Internet as their only distribution channel and ignored strategic sales planning and sales management methods to grow their businesses?

Sales management is a living, breathing animal that needs to be fed continually with new ideas and approaches to stay alive. These new ideas must be focused on the tools of generating more revenue in order to stay in business.

So, throughout this book, we are going to **look at some of the best sales management practice areas to help you and your sales team increase revenue ... because that's what it's all about.**

Business success relies on productive sales management, not the strength of the product or service you sell.

Understanding the Origins and Pillars of Integrated Pillar Management

In the current economy, the deployment of integrated sales management is the foundation of every new business success and major revenue growth. From funeral homes to theme parks, sales management is the consistent element for business controls and success. Due to this infiltration, business development opportunities continue to grow for well-managed and aggressive firms.

When integrated sales management is correctly launched, companies succeed. When incorrectly deployed, companies fail. During the Internet gold rush, from 1997 through 2000, many firms bypassed traditional business development theorems and focused instead on business hype and invalidated PR.

The key to success in today's economy is premeditated, outbound business development.

Yet, even the term "sales management" has changed. Years ago, *sales management* was a term loosely used to identify a manager who supervised a salesperson. Today, however, the term sales management has evolved into a collaborative approach combining sales, marketing, strategic alliances, and business strategy, as well as product development, into a premeditated program to generate revenue.

In traditional firms (start-ups and Fortune 1000 firms), the vice president of sales lives or dies by the success of monthly revenue plans that were forecasted twelve months earlier. They are the heroes or the goats depending on how the revenue numbers hit that month. This evaluation process is an immature method used to determine revenue success (or failure) in a firm. Often used by the CEO and investors, it ignores the fact that corporate revenue (or lack of it) can be a symptom of a greater problem with the firm's sales management program.

Firms need to focus on the integration of all of their revenue elements of management. When one singular department fails to contribute, it directly affects all corporate revenue opportunities. At that point, it is not the sales department's failure to generate revenue; it is the company's failure.

As stated earlier, the five pillars of integrated sales management in firms are sales, marketing, strategy, operations, and strategic alliances.

To succeed, you need all of these departments to be equally responsible, as partners, in revenue generation. **There can be no silos.**

If your firm has not aligned these five groups with equal compensation based on total revenues, assigned business milestones based on group performance, or implemented weekly tactical goalposts to each manager in charge of revenue-producing expectations, then it is time to change. Today, sales-focused companies can no longer afford high-priced staff executives who don't support revenue goals. Instead, you need line managers representing all departments working in concert to generate revenue.

It is not the sales department's responsibility to generate revenue—it is the company's responsibility.

As mentioned earlier, in 1986, I documented the **five-step sales management structure** to help my team and I sell $100,000 restaurant systems from an unknown, VC-funded start-up that were twice the cost of the existing market leader's product.

At that time, the firm I worked for had about 150 employees with manufacturing headquartered outside the U.S. In those days, my firm's president was a **Spin-Off/Corporate** CEO. He had managed a chain of 2,000-square-foot computer retail stores (remember this was the early 80s) in his previous position and knew nothing about selling application systems, managing outside salespeople, or the restaurant industry—but he had impressed the VCs so they gave him the job.

Chapter 1
The Complexities of Sales Management

When I made calls to the corporate office seeking support for my new five-step sales management structure, I was told they had their corporate marketing and strategy plans under way and were **not budgeted to help individual salespeople sell or sales managers manage.**

Luckily for me, the Regional VP of Sales, whom I worked for, was an entrepreneurial sort. When I approached him about my needs for the development of these five steps and explained to him that "corporate" was not responding, he just told me, "do what you need to do, Paul. Just have you and your team close business and I will approve the expenses."

So, based on my direct manager's approval, I developed the five-step sales management structure to help generate more sales.

Now, if you are an individual sales manager, I am not advocating you go off on a tangent like I did and develop your own program. Instead, hopefully, your senior management will consider the recommendations in this book as a company-wide direction.

Understanding Executive Management Types and Their Effects On Sales Management

To be a successful sales manager, you must acknowledge that you are an employee managed by an executive who is above you on the organizational chart. Understanding your boss's background, experiences, and needs will increase your success.

Here are nine types of executive management styles you may be managed by. Executives often hold a hybrid of these characteristics, so you may find more than one type that describes your boss.

1. The Engineer: Many firms evolved from a *single person engineer* business that had a technical product or service for one client within a specific business vertical. Once this product or service was installed, the engineer resold it to other like clients and launched a vertical application or service business based on the original single sale.

2. The CIO (Chief Information Officer): This executive is a better planner than the Engineer, but still comes from a technical background. CIOs are usually graduates of engineering schools and have worked in senior technical positions in other firms before they had a great idea and launched their own businesses.

3. <u>The MBA</u>: Prevalent during the dot-com craze, this founder/president usually graduated from a top MBA program and spent the last five years consulting in a big company.

4. <u>The Spin-Off/Corporate Person</u>: This management type is usually the result of a business unit spin-off of a larger, more established firm. This type also includes professional corporate managers.

5. <u>The Entrepreneur</u>: This management type usually comes from a sales or marketing background and is more focused on sales opportunities. Also, this type usually has a lot of ideas, but is not always focused.

6. <u>The Inheritor</u>: Not as prevalent today, but still active, this executive rose to the ranks through a second-generation family company, but is often not interested in the business.

7. <u>The Hybrid</u>: As many founders/managers developed skills and experiences and evolved through the other manager categories, this management type learned and evolved their skills to become a hybrid of one or more of these types.

8. <u>Family Run Business Executive</u>: This management type usually developed their

skills within the environment of the family run business. The organizational structure of the firms these executives manage is usually (although not always) designed to maximize cash flow for the principals and/or employ family members, regardless of skills.

9. <u>The Wall Street Executive</u>: This management type comes from a corporate funding, investing, or Wall Street background and focuses on business financial metrics as a key business driver in the decision-making process.

Let's take a closer look at where these individuals came from and their management skill sets. These are generic at best, but let's see if you can spot your boss.

The Engineer

Strengths

- As a salesperson, the Engineer can make a passionate, technical, and knowledgeable presentation to a prospect on a one-on-one basis.

- Based on his experiences, this person provides strong customer service for technical needs to clients.

- Because of an extensive technical background, the Engineer provides great credibility as a founder in a sales presentation.

Weaknesses
- This executive is usually a poor business planner due to his lack of experience in growing a sales and marketing department.

- The Engineer's business development process can be unfocused, with minimal specifications on engineering design, and product development occurs as he goes along.

- The Engineer does not do market research or study market demand. He assumes demand will be there for the product or service because the offering is great.

- This person doesn't do well in corporate sales presentations because Engineers are anti-corporate and uncomfortable with inquisitive questions that may be too critical of their product or service design.

- Usually Engineers display poor interpersonal and management skills and lack patience with employees who do not have the same work commitment as them. As a result, they prefer sitting by themselves in their offices, tinkering with product design rather than being in a group gathering.

The CIO

Strengths

- CIOs usually provide detailed product design on all specifications.

- CIOs are usually experienced in large groups and leading a team environment.

- CIOs understand how to make sales presentations to a corporate client.

Weaknesses

- CIOs may not understand market gap analysis.

- CIOs may not understand sales cycle mechanics and have little patience with the sales staff.

- CIOs may be corporate driven, not buyer-needs driven.

- CIOs may focus on building before selling.

The MBA

Strengths

- MBAs are experienced in business-case analysis, market studies, and product positioning.

- MBAs are comfortable with business forecasts.

- An MBA may be more of a generalist than a specialist.

- MBAs are comfortable dealing with VCs (venture capitalists, investors) and the financial community.

- MBAs are experienced in doing corporate presentations.

- MBAs may be experienced working in group environments.

Weaknesses

- MBAs may not have much hands-on experience, which leads them to focus on strategic rather than tactical deployment.

- MBAs may not understand the full-cycle sales process because they may only have half-cycle sales experience. Half-cycle salespeople are accustomed to having their firms give them leads, instead of developing leads themselves by prospecting or cold calling.

- MBAs may not understand the elements of technical product development.

- MBAs may not work well in group environments where different levels of education and experience co-exist.

- MBAs may not be experienced in handling multiple tasks simultaneously.

The Spin-Off/Corporate Person

Strengths

- This person has experience working in a team environment.

- This person has experience in business planning and forecasting.

- The Spin-Off/Corporate person has experience in marketing and sales processes.

- This person has experience making sales presentations to the corporate world.

- The Spin-Off/Corporate person may have experience working with technical specifications and development.

Weaknesses

- The Spin-Off/Corporate person may not be experienced in handling multiple tasks simultaneously (depending on the size and funding of the spin-off).

- The Spin-Off/Corporate person may not have a sales and marketing background.

- This person may not have experience selling to small companies.

- The Spin-Off/Corporate person may be too rigid in his thinking because of previous corporate restraints or experiences.

The Entrepreneur

Strengths

- Entrepreneurs have strong sales and marketing experience.

- Entrepreneurs have the ability to make presentations to small firms.

- Entrepreneurs may have an understanding of planning and funding.

- Entrepreneurs may have the ability to make presentations to large companies.

- Entrepreneurs may have experience working with teams.

Weaknesses

- Entrepreneurs may overspend on sales and marketing.

- Entrepreneurs may not invest enough time and money in product or service development.

- Entrepreneurs may not understand technical or engineering development.

- Entrepreneurs may lack the ability to focus on one specific company goal.

- Entrepreneurs may continually try to start new profit centers or businesses.

- Entrepreneurs may be too ego-driven to work in a team environment.

The Inheritor

Strengths

- Inheritors may have deep industry experience based on business longevity.

- Inheritors usually have strong sales backgrounds from personal experience in the field.

- Inheritors will usually have cross-department experience.

Weaknesses

- Inheritors may not be interested in growth and aggressive business development due to established and predictable business cash flow.

- Inheritors may not be team players with anyone outside the family.

- Inheritors may not have passion for business due to over-exposure.

The Hybrid

Strengths

- The Hybrid has experience in product or service sales and marketing.

- The Hybrid has experience in engineering project development.

- The Hybrid has experience in team management.

- The Hybrid has experience in financial management.

Weaknesses

- The Hybrid may be too much of a generalist and lack detailed knowledge of specific subject areas.

The Family Run Business Executive

Strengths

- This management ownership often offers employees a friendly, casual work environment, where individuals can succeed. Many times compensation in this organization is an unstructured offering, which allows for broad freedom when negotiating salary and commission structures.

- If this is a second generation or succeeding generation family management team, the company's financial and operational performance may be stable due to the first generation's efforts.

Weaknesses

- Family run business executives usually lack experience under traditional corporate environments. As a result, the company may not have the organizational structure needed to hold individuals accountable.

- Although the family run business may be cash rich, management may not share it with non-family members.

- Management members who are family may not be qualified to hold their current positions—jobs given to them out of nepotism—which may create a difficult environment to work in.

The Wall Street Executive

Strengths

- Driven by financial metrics, these executives are able to guide companies through stages of corporate growth and find recurring funding as needed.

- Usually well educated, the Wall Street executive often likes written reports that are logical and systematic in their recommendations, and to hear business solutions to complicated problems.

Weaknesses

- Wall Street executives often lack practical management experience and think they know everything because they have money or access to money.

- Since Wall Street executives focus primarily on key business indicators, at times the companies they manage suffer because the executives are book smart, not leadership smart.

- Compensation in companies managed by Wall Street executives is usually very structured and does not offer a broad range of negotiation options within each position's range.

These nine executive types are examined so you can better understand why many firms never fulfill their true business potential to create revenue. If you are a CEO reading this, examine your skill sets and experiences. If you are a senior sales manager, analyze your CEO's leadership, because having an integrated, outbound business plan requires commitment from the senior executive on down.

Your company's success, as well as your own, is dependent upon your senior management team embracing this concept. Understanding the background of the leadership helps everyone bypass obstacles and focus on effective methods for productive outbound revenue programs.

Chapter 1
The Complexities of Sales Management

Chapter 2

Developing a Sales Process

After reading this chapter, you will know:

- How to evaluate your sales strategy as it relates to your sales process

- How to define and evaluate your current sales process

- How to prototype your targeted prospects

- How to develop a replicable and scaleable sales process

Developing a successful, replicable, and measurable sales process is one element of growing your firm. Like six sigma models, the correct sales process should minimize and eliminate business errors that reduce your sales operational efficiencies and increase corporate profitability. Having corporate revenue success is not always the result of a proven sales process. Often individual sales successes by specific sales members are not replicable.

Successful sales processes are business maps that can be used by a broad range of sales team members over and over again. They pull up the skills of average salespeople to a corporate minimum, while helping senior salespeople expand their achievements.

Deploying and managing sales metrics is an integral part of successful management. Sales processes driven by metrics allow you to:

- Reduce your sales cycle time to close the deal

- Reduce sales capture costs per sale, including travel and expenses

- Increase your sales team's success

- Develop a training program based on factual sales needs

- Increase your sales team retention

- Increase the efficiencies of your operations, engineering, and R&D groups

Companies generally fall into one of four sales process categories:

1. A sales process based on other companies' business practices

2. A sales process based on unsubstantiated sales successes

Chapter 2
Developing a Sales Process

3. A sales process based on one salesperson's success or the selling experiences of the founder or senior manager

4. No written sales process exists at all

As firms try to grow their businesses, <u>they continue to fall backward</u> as they attempt to sell using incompatible sales models that don't work for them.

Each of these methods hinders your ability to manage salespeople and deploy a scalable and replicable sales process. Let's take a closer look.

1. **A sales process based on other companies' business practices.**

    Many times, a company will look at the sales processes of their competitors, or those described in industry trade publications, as models to emulate. They assume by this method of imitation that their firm will have the same success as these other profiled companies. But, generally, this never works because each company's product and service strengths and weaknesses are uniquely different. Additionally, the sales team competence may not be the same. For example, having a $20 million company adjust its sales process to match that of a Fortune 1000 company usually fails because the sales process of a Fortune 1000 company is not designed for revenue capture; it is designed for discipline and control.

2. **A sales process based on unsubstantiated sales successes.**

   For a sales process to work, it must be based on substantiated and documented successful sales steps and buyer profiling to maximize its effectiveness.

3. **A sales process based on one salesperson's success or the selling experiences of the founder or senior manager.**

   Just because one salesperson, or the founder of the company, has been successful selling the company's product or service, does not mean that their sales process is scalable or replicable for the average salesperson.

4. **No written sales process exists at all.**

   Today, many firms use a verbalized sales process or an implied sales process, rather than having a premeditated, documented selling process for their sales team that can be replicated on an ongoing basis.

Often, sales methodology in many companies becomes a haphazard approach, where some people sell and others don't. As I mentioned in Chapter 1, part of the reason this occurs is because many sales processes are carried over from company to company without consideration for size, product, service, sales force, or management team. This haphazard approach exists throughout the entire world, in big companies and small, start-ups and mature players.

Evaluating Your Sales Strategy

Instead of looking at sales process personalization based on the business needs of their targeted buyers, many times firms just ask each other internally what they need to do differently to change their current business outcome. Or worse, they make observations about a competitor and try to parallel those sales methods.

You see, I am not a new-wave executive who believes in the Chaos Theory, rather I believe you can reorganize your sales process with structure to generate more sales by personalizing your sales model based on your market, your firm's strengths and weaknesses, and especially your prospects' needs. A successful sales process is the sum of your corporate skills and the needs of the buyer.

You must adapt your sales process to the prospect's needs, not necessarily what worked for you or another company.

Chapter 2
Developing a Sales Process

Sales Process and Strategy Test

1. When sales revenue per salesperson is down or when your company's revenue is down, does your firm just hire more salespeople?

   ___Yes ___No

2. Have you changed your sales model during the last 24 months?

   ___Yes ___No

3. Do you have a written, documented, step-by-step sales model detailing your firm's entire sales process from pre-sale to post-sale?

   ___Yes ___No

4. When your firm discusses new sales methods, does it consult with internal peers and management only?

   ___Yes ___No

5. Does your sales team get paid the same commission for business from existing clients as business from new prospects?

   ___Yes ___No

6. Does your firm use the same sales model to sell to CFOs, CIOs, general managers, and CEOs as it does to sell to lower-level managers?

   ___Yes ___No

Chapter 2
Developing a Sales Process

7. Does your firm track closing ratios by prospect title?

   ___Yes ___No

8. Is your sales forecast/closing ratio at least 75% accurate month to month?

   ___Yes ___No

9. Is your service or product pricing reactive to your competitors?

   ___Yes ___No

10. Do your salespeople cold call at least 50 new prospects each week?

    ___ Yes ___No

11. Do you allow **only** senior executive contacts in your Customer Relationship Management or contact manager to be considered as qualified buyers when calculating your sales forecasting value (versus accepting all manager titles as valid in your sales forecast)?

    ___ Yes ___No

12. Does your sales strategy require action steps to be taken by your prospects in order to be considered qualified buyers (versus the responsive step model, where you wait for the prospect to respond to your sales communication)?

    ___ Yes ___No

Chapter 2
Developing a Sales Process

13. Does your plan offer multiple price point options to make it easier for prospects to buy (versus seeking big ticket sales opportunities driven by price)?

    ___ Yes ___ No

14. Has your firm forecasted the market demand based on research for each product and service you sell (versus a forecast based on assuming there is a demand or a market study that is more than one year old)?

    ___ Yes ___ No

15. Does your firm have a sales model that provides ongoing sales training for your team (versus a sales model where team members must educate themselves as they go)?

    ___ Yes ___ No

16. Are your firm's marketing efforts feature- or service-driven based on the superiority of your product or service (versus pain-driven based on the prospect's needs)?

    ___ Yes ___ No

17. Is your firm market-driven by trying to sell horizontally to all industries (versus vertical-driven where each product and service has an identified market, price, prospect type, business need, etc.)?

    ___ Yes ___ No

18. Does your marketing department supply ten new qualified leads each week to each sales rep?

    ___ Yes ___ No

Chapter 2
Developing a Sales Process

19. Is your sales team having a difficult time increasing sales from your existing clients?

    ___ Yes ___ No

20. Are your sales quotas the same for revenue generated from new prospects as they are from existing customers?

    ___ Yes ___ No

Correct Answers:

1) No	2) Yes	3) Yes	4) No	5) No
6) No	7) Yes	8) Yes	9) No	10) Yes
11) Yes	12) Yes	13) Yes	14) Yes	15) Yes
16) No	17) No	18) Yes	19) No	20) No

Scoring:

Each correct answer is worth 5%. How did you score? Is your score above 70%? If not, you may need a new sales process to increase revenue.

When developing a successful sales strategy, it is important to make sure that the strategy itself does not stand alone, but integrates into the corporate business plan with the appropriate execution steps. Having the right sales process strategy is the key to successful sales execution.

**Sales strategy first.
Sales success second!**

Sales strategy is not just a verbal commitment to execute. It is also a detailed written guideline used by management and staff to correctly implement the business strategy based on a specific sales model. **If your sales strategy is vague or not detailed enough, your sales execution will fail!**

Since compensation plans of sales staff and management should be tied directly to their ability to hit sales quotas, the sales strategy must be consistent with the team's ability to implement the sales process based on detailed logic and selling guidelines.

Your sales team cannot implement a sales process if the strategic groundwork has not been carefully developed or does not match your firm's current operating business model needs, sales team capabilities, or delivery capabilities. **A sales process cannot be based on management's forecasted hope. It must be based on <u>researched strategic logic</u>.**

Developing a Replicable and Scaleable Sales Process

To develop a replicable, scalable sales process that works with the majority of your sales team requires you to understand how and why your prospects buy.

Chapter 2
Developing a Sales Process

To accomplish this, you need to prototype your targeted or current buyer, evaluate your current sales process, and determine your sales goals by:

1. Understanding why prospects buy from you.
2. Understanding why you lose business.
3. Learning how to show "visual value."
4. Documenting your sales process step-by-step.
5. Quantifying your prospect prototype.
6. Determining the fully loaded cost of one sale before corporate general and administrative (G&A) costs.
7. Developing your sales metric benchmarks for success.
8. Documenting your top ten sales objections with responses.
9. Training your sales team regularly; role-play often.
10. Making cold calling a requirement.
11. Providing a market potential of at least 300 prospects per salesperson.
12. Developing quotas that are accurate.

Chapter 2
Developing a Sales Process

13. Evaluating salespeople on metrics, not emotion.

14. Assigning a maximum of 3 business industry verticals to each salesperson.

15. Using lost sales analysis as a business tool.

Let's jump right in and talk about prototyping your targeted prospects, evaluating your current sales process, and determining your sales goals.

Prototyping Your Targeted Prospects

Knowing your buyers is the key to selling more. Not knowing your buyers or their specific sales characteristics reduces your success. To prototype your buyer, research these areas:

1. How does your product or service increase income, decrease expenses, or manage risks for the prospect?

2. How does your product or service create value for the prospect?

3. What are the business consequences if the prospect does not buy from you or another qualified vendor?

4. What are the prospect titles that sign your contracts (VPs of Finance, VPs of Marketing, general managers, CEOs, etc.)?

5. What is the average dollar value of your first sale to a prospect (by industry)?

6. What are the top five business industries you sell into?

7. What is the average annual revenue of the companies you sell to?

8. What is your geographic selling zone (nationwide, local, etc.)?

9. Calculate the average discount you give to a prospect—by title and industry?

10. Calculate the average discount you give to a new prospect versus an existing customer?

11. Determine the average length of time it takes to sell each prospect by title, industry, and buying option.

Evaluating Your Current Sales Process

Knowing your current sales process will help you understand how your team currently operates, where the gaps are, and what is needed to build a replicable and scalable sales process. You will want to research these areas:

1. What is the five-year value of a client after the first sale?

2. Review all sales for the last 24 months and calculate your top ten accounts by revenue

and what total percentages they contributed to overall corporate and department revenue.

3. Review all sales staff success for the last 24 months and determine the percentage of success for sales to new prospects versus sales to existing customers: a) by individual salesperson, and b) by the team as a whole.

4. Determine the average sales experience, in years, of the top 10% of your sales team.

5. Document the top ten sales objections your sales team hears from prospects by title, industry, and annual revenue.

6. Determine what questioning techniques your sales team currently uses to determine when a prospect is a qualified buyer.

7. Based on your sales success, determine the method used to generate leads that resulted in closed deals during the last 24 months (cold calling, networking, marketing, etc.).

8. Review all of your sales during the last 24 months and determine what percentage of deals required your management team to meet with the prospect to close the business.

9. Ascertain and document the sales steps needed to close a product or service sale (cold call, first meeting, discovery meeting,

presentation, proposal development, proposal submittal, etc.).

10. Determine the cost for each lead provided to your sales team (total corporate new revenue generated for one year divided by total number of leads generated by marketing = cost per lead).

Determining Your Sales Goals

Current sales models and current prototype buyers may not be the targeted prospects your company is seeking to sell. At times, salespeople take the path of least resistance and sell to prospects they feel comfortable selling to, not necessarily who you, as management, want them to sell.

To develop your structured sales process, you must measure the gap between your current sales model, your current prospect prototype, and your corporate selling goals. If there is no gap, then (and only then) you can develop your sales process.

If there is a gap between your current sales success and your sales prospect objectives, then you must reduce the gap to help your sales team focus on the company's needs . . . not their needs.

- Is your sales team selling to the targeted prospects you wish them to sell?

- Does your sales team focus on the right prospect title?

Chapter 2
Developing a Sales Process

- Is your sales team only selling to existing customers?

With the data from these questions, you can develop and write your sales process.

Pulling It All Together and Documenting Your Sales Process

Once you have prototyped your targeted prospects and current sales model, you can now integrate these two resources into a written sales process that helps your sales team understand your model and the expectations you have for them to sell.

Your sales process is the framework from which you and your sales team both operate; and it should be in a written format. Once the sales process is documented, it should be used as a tool to teach and manage your sales team. Your sales process must:

1. Describe who your targeted industries are and what their annual revenues are.

2. Identify the title of the targeted prospect.

3. Describe the products and services you expect your sales team to sell.

4. Describe the targeted average price per sale for each product and service you sell (gross profit or gross margin).

5. Describe the anticipated sales objections the sales rep can expect to hear from each industry they sell to and from each prospect title they are expected to sell.

6. List each sales step expected for each product and service you sell.

7. List how your sales team must qualify prospects at each sales step to determine if they should continue working with the prospect.

8. Identify the anticipated length of time it should take to close a sale from beginning to end.

9. Identify sales metric benchmarks for success.

10. Determine the expectations of lead generation (i.e., cold calling, networking, marketing, etc.).

11. Describe when and how often the company will provide sales training.

Once you have gathered this information, pull it all together in a document that you can provide to your sales team, and as needed, to your management team. You should review your sales process twice a year to make sure it is relevant to the current selling environment you operate in.

Chapter 2
Developing a Sales Process

Chapter 3

Organizing the Structure of Your Sales Team

After reading this chapter, you will know:

- How to evaluate and categorize your sales team by personality type

- How to determine your company's business growth stage

- Which personalities are needed for specific stages of business growth

- How to maximize key account success using a team approach

The organizational design of your sales team is dependent on five variables:

1. The personality types of the salespeople you currently employ

2. The corporate sales growth goals of your company

3. The number of salespeople currently in your company

4. The complexity of your product or service offering

5. The length of the sales cycle for your average sale

Understanding Sales Personality Types

The goal for any sales manager is to produce the greatest sales volume at the lowest sales capture cost, while managing the unique personalities of the sales team. Having managed all types of salespeople, I have found the key is to balance revenue with personalities, though it is always a challenge.

Below, I have identified **eight types of sales personalities** common to many sales teams. There are two primary types—Hunters and Farmers—and six hybrid types which are Players, Cowboys, Politicians, Trotters, Half-Cycle Salespeople and Non-Performers.

Hunters

Characteristics:

These reps are full-cycle salespeople, are motivated by money and success, and will out-work all others to be number one. These reps always penetrate new prospects.

Background:

Often, these reps are experienced account managers who understand the concept of a full sales cycle. They may have previously come from an aggressive outbound sales force where achievement and competitiveness were expected. These reps focus on a prospect's business needs and selling business results, not features or functions. Hunters will do what it takes to be the number one sales rep and will cold call. In addition to **being low maintenance and team players for management,** Hunters are usually well liked by their clients and peers. Lastly, these salespeople are constant students of new sales methods and always invest in their own sales education.

Farmers

Characteristics:

These reps usually hang on to existing customers or key accounts or house accounts and milk the sales quota with minimal effort.

Background:

Usually these reps have been assigned, or inherited, premium revenue accounts that are on autopilot and generate enough income for these salespeople to be acceptable and keep them on or near quota without much effort. These reps may be experienced full-cycle salespeople, but feel there is no need to expand their customer base because of the steady spending habits of their existing accounts. Another belief Farmers have in common is that they deserve this "gravy train" because they may have originally sold the account after several years of mining. They are **always low maintenance** for sales management and these individuals just want to be left alone (and hidden) from management reporting responsibilities. They like their expense account and talking about establishing long-term relationships with clients. They often will not let management meet with their house account contacts, explaining "it's a delicate situation, very political, and they have it under control."

Players

Characteristics:

These reps are consistently at or near sales quota and follow all company programs.

Background:

Although they are never the top salespeople, Players will never be at the bottom and are consistent in their performance day in and day out. These reps are team players, understand the game of sales, and are well-spoken account managers. These reps are well liked by management and customers, and are **very low maintenance for management.**

Cowboys

Characteristics:

These reps are usually top performers in quota, very verbal, and have many years of sales experience.

Background:

Normally, these reps have multiple years of successful sales experience with other companies. Usually they do not stay at any firm longer than two years due to burning too many bridges with executives. Cowboys may outsell other types of sales reps, but they are always **high maintenance** for sales management. These individuals do not like paperwork, company procedures, or sales meetings. Most deals that are closed by Cowboys will have complications on pricing, payment terms, and verbal commitments on product or service deliverables. They will usually do or say anything to close the deal. Often they are not team players and will be destructive to the sales group. Customers may like these reps at the beginning of the sales cycle, but lose faith when promises made during the proposal stage do not come to fruition after the sale. Some customers will totally despise this type of account manager. Cowboys may appear to be too slick for large major account sales and may be weak on a true understanding of the complexities of the product or service you sell. Often these individuals feel they need no management.

Politicians

Characteristics:

These reps are usually high sales quota and target performers. Politicians want a sales management job or are looking for ways to under-cut sales department policies to reposition themselves more favorably in front of senior management.

Background:

These account executives can be a combination of Cowboy and Farmer personalities, but are usually higher performers who use company politics as a weapon. If these reps have more Cowboy characteristics, they will always use their performance as a measurement of why their sales methods are better. In small privately held companies, these reps are always going to the CEO for one thing or another. In large firms, Politicians interact quickly with VPs to build a consensus on their sales processes and to "prove" their way is better. These account executives are *always* high maintenance **for sales management** and they are usually **not well liked** by fellow salespeople. Generally, they will not do paperwork on time, are not team players, and cannot be trusted.

Trotters

Characteristics:

These reps are new salespeople, learning the steps to successfully close business and are generally hard workers.

Background:

Usually, Trotters have two years or less of sales experience in the same industry or may have sold different services or products in other markets before coming to your company. They are well liked by management and customers and work as hard as **Hunters (who are often their mentors).** They will usually hit 80% or better of assigned sales quotas and will increase their closing ratio as time goes on. They follow management guidelines and are always seeking information on how to be a better salesperson. They are **medium maintenance for sales management,** but time spent with these reps is a good investment since they often become Hunters.

Half-Cycle Salespeople

Characteristics:

These reps feel they are senior salespeople who are above basic sales skills, like cold calling, account management paperwork, and being team players.

Background:

Usually these reps have evolved from one of two backgrounds. **Background A,** in which they do not have a lot of sales experience, but have other business knowledge. Additionally, they are not accustomed to the concept of a full-cycle sale. **Background B,** in which they have sales experience, but previous sales managers never required them to actively hunt for new business using an outbound sales process. These reps focus on the perception that "client visits" equals "relationship building." Often they have been financially successful in previous positions, which led them to believe they are senior sales executives. (The size of a paycheck is not always a sign of good salesmanship.) **Usually, half-cycle salespeople are low maintenance** for management as long as they are not asked to cold call prospects and are given enough leads from in-house marketing programs. These reps are usually fair negotiators, but prefer to maintain a low profile inside the sales team so management will not bother them.

Non-Performers

Characteristics:

These reps are low performers for hitting sales quotas or their targets. They try hard and are well liked by all.

Background:

Usually, Non-Performers do not have sales ability or previous sales experience. They are incorrectly positioned in the wrong type of job. Although liked by all and quick to follow management direction, they are **normally high maintenance** because of their inability to qualify clients and the need for maximum support during the sales cycle. Non-Performers may be better off in a sales support position, interacting with the sales team and clients in a non-sales role.

While there are many types of sales reps, we have explored the most typical personalities that seem to be pervasive in companies large and small. These characteristics, although general in nature, will be recognized by any experienced sales manager and should be used as guidelines when analyzing sales team members that work for you.

Often salespeople exhibit several characteristics in their personalities of the eight personality types. Giving independent psychological tests to your salespeople can be helpful in understanding why they act certain ways. The sales personality review is also a quick assessment to help match your current sales team's selling habits and characteristics with your sales goals.

Chapter 3
Organizing the Structure of Your Sales Team

The first question every sales manager needs to consider is "what are the characteristics of my current team and, ideally, what kind of team members should I look for when I hire new sales staff?"

There is no specific answer, but I will give you some guidelines based on my experience and the potential needs of your firm.

To accomplish this, use the following worksheet to list all of your sales reps by their sales personality type. If you have reps that are hybrids, pick their dominant traits. If you have some who do not fit any of these general categories, then make up your own categories.

Chapter 3
Organizing the Structure of Your Sales Team

Current Sales Team Member Worksheet

List your salespeople based on their sales personality type.

Hunters:
1._____
2._____
3._____
4._____
5._____

Farmers:
1._____
2._____
3._____
4._____
5._____

Players:
1._____
2._____
3._____
4._____
5._____

Cowboys:
1._____
2._____
3._____
4._____
5._____

Politicians:
1._____
2._____
3._____
4._____
5._____

Half-Cycle Salespeople:
1._____
2._____
3._____
4._____
5._____

Trotters:
1._____
2._____
3._____
4._____
5._____

Non-Performers:
1._____
2._____
3._____
4._____
5._____

Determining Your Company's Business Life Cycle

Once you have classified your sales team by personality types, you need to determine your company's (or department's or region's) sales growth model.

When looking at your sales staff, try to match your product or service's current life cycle with your sales team's abilities and personalities. This approach of matching sales staff with your firm's business revenue growth needs can be implemented for the company as a whole, for unique products or services you sell, or for separate sales departments. In fact, you can have different products or services going through different business cycles and have different sales personalities for each.

Generally, a life cycle of a company, product, or service falls into four basic phases, which include:

1. **Innovative stage.** In the innovative stage of a young company or new product offering, cash flow and/or market share is king. **Usually this is a firm with a product or service that is less than two years old, though it could be older.** Often this is an educational sales cycle for buyers, where you have to explain your business value to them. Usually there are few competitors at this stage.

Chapter 3
Organizing the Structure of Your Sales Team

2. **Growth stage.** The growth stage occurs between two to four years into the life cycle. The firm has often succeeded in establishing a market position for its offering, so it is time to capture tremendous amounts of revenue (or gross margin) growth. At this stage, often the business value is identifiable to buyers. Competition enters the market at this time, now that the market has been proven viable by innovative stage players.

3. **Mature or plateau stage.** The mature or plateau stage occurs between four to ten years into the life cycle. The firm is selling products or services that are in a tight, competitive (commodity-based) market, where the advantage is not readily identifiable (other than price). At this stage, the business value is standardized and not perceived to be unique. Lots of competitors at this stage.

4. **Decline stage.** The decline stage generally occurs after ten years. If the firm or product is in a reduced demand cycle, with a shrinking competitor pool, the firm may have entered into the decline stage of its life cycle. In this stage, the business value is being reduced by newer buyer options. Competitors are decreasing as they seek new markets with greater growth opportunities.

It is important to match your sales staff to the current life cycle of your firm, product, or service. Each of the sales types listed has positive and negative attributes and their skill sets need to be matched appropriately to your firm's business model needs.

Having all **Cowboys** or all **Trotters** can adversely affect your sales success because, at times, *you need both*.

Managing salespeople on a daily basis can be challenging. You need to understand their background, their needs, and your firm's current market position and revenue goals. All of these elements must blend and match.

When your sales team's skill sets and personalities do not match your firm's current sales model requirements, you then have an unproductive sales team and ultimately an expensive sales capture process.

Sales departments often miss quota attainment because there is a mismatch of skill sets to the company's current life cycle, or senior management has allowed unproductive sales types (like Political and Half-Cycle) to dominate the sales team. If you are the senior person responsible for sales management, analyze your sales team and your firm's current life cycle, and then match them accordingly.

This is the <u>fastest method to reaching sales quota</u> for your sales team.

Matching Business Life Cycle with Personality Types

Each stage of business benefits by certain types of salespeople. The only two types that I do not list below are Half-Cycle salespeople and Non-Performers simply because I do not recommend them in any firm that wants to sustain their current revenue or grow revenue.

Here are my recommendations of the types of salespeople you should hire based on each stage of your product or service's life cycle:

Innovation Stage

Sales Types Needed

50% Hunters
25% Cowboys
25% Players

For this stage, you will generally need **Hunters** and **Cowboys** to find business opportunities, explain your business value, and generate cash. Although Cowboys are high-maintenance sales reps, they will generate business and spur higher performance by Hunters and Players. The best way to manage Cowboys is to feed their egos and double-check **every contract** they present to make sure it is clean.

During this stage, your firm should not have the patience or the luxury of having **Non-Performers, Half-Cycle,** or **Farmer** salespeople.

Growth Stage

Sales Types Needed

60% Hunters
20% Players
10% Trotters
10% Cowboys

In this stage, your firm has succeeded in establishing its market position and business value, so it is time to capture tremendous amounts of revenue growth. You need a majority of Hunters and Players who will sell aggressively, with minimal maintenance by management.

Trotters (Hunters in training) are also needed as you build your sales program for the long-term. Cowboys (needed less now) are still important to keep everyone on their toes, but they must increase sales results year over year to balance their high-maintenance requirements.

Mature Stage

Sales Types Needed

50% Players
30% Trotters
10% Hunters
10% Farmers

As you enter this stage, you need to reduce your sales operating costs to maintain corporate profitability. Since selling in this stage is less difficult, there is no need to have a disproportionate share of highly compensated and senior salespeople, like Hunters and Cowboys, because your firm is well entrenched and stable. If you have correctly positioned your company in the marketplace, you would be overpaying the Hunters and Cowboys to sell quota that Players and Trotters can capture for you at a reduced sales expense.

Decline Stage

Sales Types Needed

50% Hunters
30% Cowboys
20% Players

If your firm is now selling products or services that are in a highly competitive (commodity-based) market, where your advantage is not readily identifiable, your sales staff requirements have come full circle.

You do not need Trotters or Farmers. Instead, you need an aggressive outbound sales staff that will extend your life cycle until you establish a new product or service and start the whole process again. Your sales expenses will increase at this stage as you deploy your outbound sales Hunters.

Market Growth Alignment

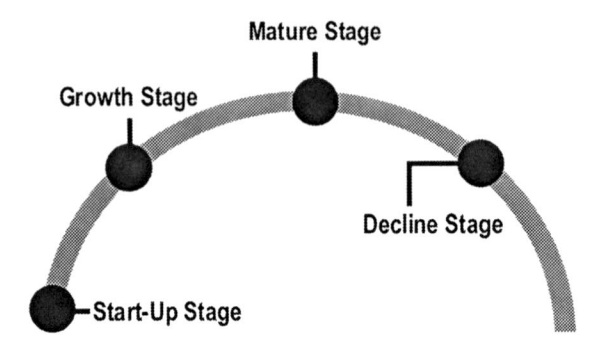

- Mature Stage
- Growth Stage
- Decline Stage
- Start-Up Stage

Match your sales team members' personality types with your business cycles and you will sell more. Keep the same salespeople year after year, regardless of their skills, and your sales may suffer.

Types of Sales Team Positions

Your team's organizational structure will usually have a mix of sales positions based on your company and the needs of your offerings. The key to increasing your sales team's organizational success is to develop an outbound sales team structure that dedicates *a portion of your team to selling to existing customers and the remaining salespeople selling to new prospects.*

1. **Direct Salespeople/Account Managers for New Business.** These salespeople are responsible for direct sales of your products and services and have an assigned sales quota, business industry, or target goal. They

are usually paid a base salary or draw (depending on the industry) and a commission and/or bonus plan based on personal sales in their assigned territories.

2. **Direct Salespeople/Account Managers for Existing Business.** These salespeople are responsible for direct sales of your products and services and have an assigned sales quota or target goal. They are usually paid a base salary or draw (depending on the industry) and a commission and/or bonus plan based on personal sales in their assigned territories.

3. **Key Account or Major Account Salespeople.** These salespeople are usually assigned designated accounts by geography, business vertical, or account names. They are paid a base salary and commission or bonus based on sales success.

4. **Corporate Overlay Account Managers.** These salespeople are used by large firms that sell multiple products and services to the same Global 2000 company. Often overlay managers sell at a national level and work in tandem with other account managers who sell business units at a local level. They are sometimes called Business Development Managers.

5. **Account Pursuit Team.** These salespeople are usually a sub-segment sales team of Key Account Managers who group together to aggressively sell to a specific targeted account as a premeditated process.

6. **Sales Engineers or Technical Sales Support Specialists.** Although traditionally not direct salespeople, these individuals often act as team members with account managers (common in technical and engineering companies).

7. **Business Development Account Managers.** These account managers focus on signing up strategic resellers who generate revenue for the firm. (They are often also used in government sales where sales cycles are a cross between sales and long-term business development.)

8. **Channel/Resellers Managers.** These salespeople usually have dedicated sales accounts, and typically set up either new strategic partner relationships or authorized resellers.

Oftentimes salespeople are paid the same compensation for selling to existing customers as they are for selling to new prospects, but I don't recommend this. To increase the success of your sales process, pay salespeople based on their job's specific contribution to increasing corporate profitability. Chapter 5 discusses compensation in greater detail, but here are some guidelines to consider with regard to compensation and quota expectations:

1. Assign different compensation plans and salespeople to sell to new prospects versus to existing customers.

2. If you can't classify your sales team members as Hunters and Farmers, then use a hybrid model and assign each salesperson a quota for business from new prospects and a separate quota for business from existing customers.

3. When building your sales organizational chart, understand that business development is a long sales cycle. Business development reps should be assigned a sales quota based on their resellers' revenue goals, not just how many partners they sign up.

4. Generally speaking, the more complex your sales cycle or offering is, the more layers of support you will have (overlay salespeople). Tie their compensation to the success in helping the sale proceed to the next step.

5. If you use an inside sales team to generate inbound sales leads, link them to the sales generated by the outside sales team's success with the leads in which they provide.

Using the Pursuit Sales Team Model to Maximize Key Account Success

One way for companies to maximize key account success is by developing "pursuit sales teams" for key and targeted major accounts.

The pursuit sales team model is a structured strategic sales process that focuses on generating specific revenue from one company based on a premeditated selling process. Often used for large national and international company sales, its methodology also holds well for smaller company sales.

The pursuit sales team approach uses your firm's collective sales, marketing, and strategy knowledge to analyze key sales opportunities and determine the appropriate way to sell to targeted accounts.

1. **Select pursuit team members.**
   The selection of a pursuit sales team is the basic foundation of any major account success. Questions will be raised, such as: Should an account manager who is located within the geography of a key account's corporate headquarters be part of the team? Should marketing and operations personnel be included as part of the pursuit sales team? Does your vice president of sales have to be part of the pursuit team? Selling in this team environment requires a subordination of ego, and sometimes title, to determine the best

distribution of talent to help your firm sell. Always pick skill sets from operations, sales, and management to form the nucleus of your pursuit sales team.

2. **Develop the pursuit sales team's preliminary strategy.**
Selling to targeted accounts requires an individualized sales approach, which starts as a perception of the prospect's business needs and ends with their actual needs that are determined during a later discovery phase. Using a cookie-cutter sales process based on similar key account experiences or previous sales into this existing account will only minimize your success. When selling to targeted accounts, each sale and each executive buyer has his own buying criteria, which can change deal by deal. Custom fit your preliminary sales strategy to what you are trying to sell, the firm you are selling to, and the business needs of the executive who signs the purchase order.

3. **Identify your firm's sales value proposition.**
One of the first questions I ask senior management teams is why a prospect should buy from them. In most cases, the response is "We have the best product or service" or "We are the best company when it comes to customer service." These replies sound as

Chapter 3
Organizing the Structure of Your Sales Team

unique as vanilla ice cream. To sell to key accounts, you must know why prospects will buy from you instead of your competitors.[2]

4. **Identify why you may not sell the targeted account.**
   All of us like to believe that when a key account is presented a compelling reason to buy a product or service, there is a logical reason for them to decide not to buy it. But, selling is not a logical process—it requires a premeditated sales process to help you limit bottlenecks. Senior management never buys on price, features, or functions. Senior management always buys on their impression of your business value. During Phase 1 (pre-sales engagement phase), analyze why you might not sell the key account and manage the sales objections before they happen.

5. **Identify key account contacts to be targeted.**
   It is quite common for key account sales methods to focus on one contact entry point. This is a serious mistake. When trying to sell to strategic accounts through a pursuit sales team approach, always make multiple senior management contacts, at the same time, to increase your odds of penetration. When

---
[2] Covered in detail in my book, *Value Forward Selling: How to Sell to Management* located at www.howtoselltomanagement.com.

launching into a new account, seek parallel sales paths to maximize your sales success. Relying on only one contact will minimize your sales success.

6. **Plan your meeting and develop talking points.**
The use of a pursuit sales team requires the development of specific tactical talking point guidelines for all members of the selling team to use in harmony as an integrated sales approach. Have you ever sat in a key account sales meeting with senior management prospects when one of your team members says the wrong thing? This usually happens because there is a psychological need for team members to feel as though they contributed to the sales process, so they respond inadvertently and say something inappropriate. When focusing on key accounts, ALWAYS provide typed talking points for all of the team members so everyone knows what should and should NOT be said.

7. **Identify methods that will be used to reach targeted key contacts on the first introduction.**
Now that you have developed your team strategy, created talking points, and identified your entry positions, you must now decide how your first foray into the key

account will be accomplished. Will it be a cold call or an introduction by a business partner? Will you network or are you going to have a lower-level manager introduce you? Each one of these processes has an impact on later sales phases and needs to be weighed selectively. Senior management paints "visual brochures" about you and your firm based on what words you use and how they are introduced to them the first time. So, always paint your visual brochure in a positive way on the first contact. It could be your last contact.

Pursuit Sales Team Process Model

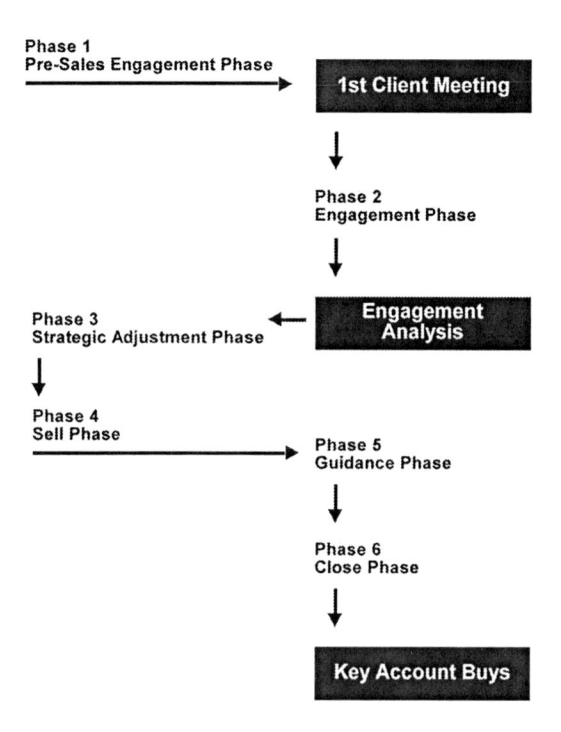

```
Phase 1
Pre-Sales Engagement Phase  →  [1st Client Meeting]
                                      ↓
                               Phase 2
                               Engagement Phase
                                      ↓
Phase 3                    ←   [Engagement Analysis]
Strategic Adjustment Phase
    ↓
Phase 4
Sell Phase  →  Phase 5
               Guidance Phase
                      ↓
               Phase 6
               Close Phase
                      ↓
               [Key Account Buys]
```

Phase 1 – Select your team. Prepare your value position. Create your talking points. Know why the prospect will buy or not buy.

Phase 2 – Contact multiple key account entry points. Present your value. Determine the prospects' business needs.

Phase 3 – Reassess and adjust your strategic positional value based on your client discovery and discussions. Reconfirm they are qualified buyers.

Phase 4 – Enter the sell phase by presenting your offering to management in detail.

Phase 5 – Interact with management contacts and identified department manager liaisons for sales guidance on your positional value on why they should buy from you or not buy. Adjust your approach as needed.

Phase 6 – You are successful. The prospect buys once. Determine how to move from a transactional sale (1st sale) to a relationship sale (2nd sale) with this key account.

Chapter 4

Hiring the Right Salespeople

After reading this chapter, you will know:

- Why most salespeople are not full-cycle salespeople
- How to find good salespeople using a non-traditional method
- How to select candidates based on your needs and their life cycle
- How to evaluate candidates more effectively
- Why you should invest in sales training and sales incentives
- How to manage cultural performance
- What to include in sales job descriptions

Full-Cycle Salespeople versus Half-Cycle Salespeople

Finding, training, and maintaining an effective sales staff gets harder every day.

Chapter 4
Hiring the Right Salespeople

In many cases, salespeople are over paid and are what I call "half-cycle" salespeople.

Strong statement . . . but true.

So, what is a half-cycle salesperson? Although I discussed half-cycle salespeople briefly in the previous chapter, I am going to expand on that discussion here.

Most salespeople have never been held accountable or been taught how to aggressively hunt for new prospects, professionally communicate business value, negotiate contracts, or close deals. Often these salespeople believe meeting numerous times with prospects means they are creating "relationships" and that these visits will force the prospects to shorten their sales cycles, eliminate competitors, and make them buy from them. This lack of full sales cycle skills is called "half-cycle sales."

Often, these salespeople expect their management team to feed them an overabundant supply of qualified leads, pay them more money than they are worth, and accept sales success that is less than expected.

More than ever, it is difficult to find salespeople who are full-cycle sales professionals. Instead, many salespeople excel at one phase of a full-cycle sales process, while their overall sales skill set is insufficient.

So, who are full-cycle salespeople?

Full-cycle salespeople hunt for new business, communicate business value to management, negotiate client sales objections, and close business by themselves.

Why is it hard to find good full-cycle salespeople?

- Hiring good salespeople for a growth company is a full-time job.

- Most salespeople today did not plan to have a career in sales. They majored in math, biology, history, or political science in college (or alternatively didn't go to college), but ended up in sales because of multiple job changes or a desire to earn more money.

- Ongoing sales training is often talked about, but almost non-existent in privately held companies and minimally delivered in public companies.

- Most companies do not have a written sales process that is replicable and measures sales staff efficiencies.

- Many salespeople do not invest in their own sales education.

- Most companies do not integrate sales, marketing, and strategy to help the sales team sell more successfully. Struggling to succeed, salespeople have become highly mobile in their job positions, always looking for better sales opportunities.

- Most salespeople view themselves as being self-employed, where time is theirs to assign or waste as they see fit (regardless of whether the person is receiving a salary as a full-time employee).

- After a salesperson becomes financially comfortable (usually a base salary or advanced draw amount), it is not uncommon to find him falling into a cruise mode because he is not motivated by other company achievement or compensation programs.

- Most salespeople will not cold call because they believe it is below their seniority level.

So, finding and keeping the full-cycle salespeople is difficult. It is an issue that has many variables which management often can't control.

One variable that is controllable is trying to match the personality of the person you need to hire with the personality of the candidate you are interviewing.

Hiring a salesperson is a one-year commitment. You may not keep that person for one year, but the time you invest, which includes the probationary period and termination, will affect your sales quota for a fiscal year if they are not successful.

Finding Good Salespeople

Where do you find good salespeople?

Finding good salespeople is always a challenge. You can use want ads, headhunters, and online Internet databases, but everybody else uses these too. The best way to find good salespeople is by **attending industry trade shows and local business trade shows**. Trade shows allow you to observe how salespeople work, dress, and interact with prospects—without them knowing they are being observed.

Go to a trade show, walk around, and watch how salespeople behave in their booths. Some stand with their hands in their pockets, others have hangovers from too much playing the night before, and then there are those who just ignore prospects as they walk by.

Where else can you unobtrusively observe salespeople in the selling process without them knowing it?

Go to a trade show, watch, and take notes. Interact with booth salespeople, collect business cards, then follow up with prospective sales candidates later in the week. This is a great and inexpensive way to recruit a strong sales team.

Hiring Salespeople Based on Your Business Needs

Interviewing and hiring successful full-cycle salespeople is never easy. Even in a slow economy, the pool of talent is geometrically larger, but it is still challenging to find the right candidates to fit your current business needs.

In my experience, what works best and will maximize your sales success is to **match the needs and sales experiences of the candidate's life cycle** with your company's **business life cycle**.

While résumés, references, W-2s, personal contact lists, salesmanship, and product and service knowledge skill sets contribute to the candidate's measurement of success, the number one element I consider is life cycle.

I define *life cycle* as the candidate's current stage (not age) in life with regard to what she wants to achieve both personally and professionally. Having a "stand up and look at me" résumé may get my attention, but it does not tell me how much she will sell for the next three years. What a person did yesterday, does not always tell me what she may do today or tomorrow.

If a person's résumé shows that she is a Fortune 1000 salesperson who earned $100,000 last year, this does not confirm that she will exert the same amount of commitment and passion in my $45 million a year, privately held company. On the surface, I might assume she will be an awesome candidate, but her life cycle might totally contradict this perception.

In fact, this new major account manager may be taking the job to live on a $100K base and float into a $200K annual income. This lack of potential success doesn't show up on résumés or reference checks, but it becomes obvious after 90 days and after you've paid the headhunter fee for a fireball account manager who is just a shooting star that has burned out.

Give me a candidate who recently bought an expensive home or one who is going from a two-income to a single-income household, because she will sell quota every time. The easiest way to discover the life-cycle attributes of sales candidates is by taking them out to dinner and chatting with them about their interests and goals.

Listed below are some key life-cycle characteristics to look for when hiring a salesperson. Although the traditional elements of sales candidate qualifications are important, these life-cycle positions will help confirm their passions and motivations.

Chapter 4
Hiring the Right Salespeople

When possible, seek candidates who:

- are the sole source of household income
- have expensive hobbies
- enjoy extracurricular sports, but don't allow this to interfere with work
- own their own home or want to buy a new home

By reviewing a candidate's life cycle as part of your interviewing criteria, you will help minimize an incorrect selection of targeted sales candidates.

Another characteristic, although not necessarily reflective of a person's current life cycle, is whether she comes from a large family and/or played sports in high school. If so, then this person is likely to be competitive in nature.

Someone recently asked me how I can evaluate a person's potential sales performance based on their athletic background, current lifestyle, or hobbies. My answer: a Hunter or Trotter does not give 200% energy only 50% of the day. People usually give all or nothing 100% of the time. If a person is a Hunter or Trotter at work, she is probably the same in her personal life.

Are these absolute rules? Of course not, but as a sales executive trying to make the right hiring decision, you have to carefully weigh all

Chapter 4
Hiring the Right Salespeople

employment information on a candidate's résumé and, **yes, I dare say,** make a judgment call on the person. In today's protected employment market, it can be very difficult to get a straightforward reference because of all the restrictions on what employers can say about former employees.

By the time you interview and hire a new salesperson, usually 1-3 months have gone by. Then you're going to give them 3-6 months to succeed. If they are failing, most firms put salespeople on a probation period of 1-2 months. If you let them go, then you have to start the cycle all over again to find a replacement.

When hiring salespeople, it is a one-year commitment for the employer.

When the wrong salesperson is hired, the cost is somewhere between $10,000 and $60,000 or more a month. That's right, $10,000 to $60,000 A MONTH when they don't sell. This includes salary, benefits, travel and expenses, and, possibly, a headhunter placement fee, as well as the **cost of sales they did not capture during their employment tenure**. In addition, this does not cover sales management expense wasted on non-productive salespeople.

Remember, when you budget for a new salesperson in your department or company, you base this investment expense on the amount of gross revenue or gross margin you expect him to contribute to your firm. Thus, if he doesn't sell, you must consider the loss of sales capture as the total true cost to your company. This calculation is provided in detail under a section entitled Calculating Lost Sales Analysis in Chapter 9.

So, be tough when evaluating candidates. Here are ten guidelines I always use when evaluating potential salespeople. I award 10% for each and the person must get a minimum of 60% to make it to my short list.

Evaluating Candidates

Guideline One—Income Verification

I assume all good salespeople will try to sell me, but one way to confirm their sales success is by reviewing their W-2s. During the first interview, I ask how much compensation they made the previous year and how it was calculated. Then, during the second or third interview (if they make it that far), I ask to see documentation. Always ask to see the person's W-2 or income verification for the last three years.

If they squirm, it usually means they misrepresented how much they made, the amount of their base, or their true commission plan. I have had some candidates argue that it was private information. Yes, it is private, but if you are telling me that **X** amount is your current income plan, then you have already made it public, so it becomes a matter of confirmation. To those individuals who insist that it is private, I respond, "Just provide a copy of your W-2 and black out everything except your base and commissions." You may be surprised at what you discover.

I once had a salesperson hand me a Salesperson of the Year trophy, as an example of his success, during our first interview. After due diligence, I discovered he had actually purchased the award from a local trophy store and had his name inscribed on it. The truth was, he had been fired from his last sales job for lack of success.

Here are some sample interview questions you might consider adding to your evaluation process:

> **Interview Question:** Did you hit your sales quota (target) the last 2 years or more?
>
> **Correct Answer:** Yes
>
> Hiring a salesperson is a one-year commitment. Why hire someone who failed at another company? Yes, there are sometimes valid reasons for not selling one's quota, but with such a high cost for salespeople, minimize your risk by hiring successful people, not people who have too many explanations. Good salespeople always figure a way to hit quota, regardless of the company's product, service, pricing, or market issues.

Interview Question: Did you make your quota by selling to new prospects?

Correct Answer: Yes

The candidate should make at least 50% of her current sales quota selling to new prospects. Selling to existing customers is always easier than selling to new prospects. Hire salespeople who can penetrate new accounts. Many salespeople hit their sales quotas by hibernating with existing customers and then think they are senior salespeople (Farmers).

Guideline Two—Evaluate Impression

Always evaluate a candidate from the client's viewpoint and consider the impression the candidate leaves with you. Did the person send a letter confirming your interview? Was the candidate on time? Did he send a thank-you card for the meeting? Did the candidate ask for a second appointment at the end of the first interview? If the candidate was stuck in traffic, did he call ahead and say he was running late? Did the candidate research your company or at least look at your website? Remember, how the person treats you is a reflection of how he will treat your prospects when you are not monitoring his sales skills.

Guideline Three—Look for Experience in a Similar Company Size

Find out if the candidate is currently working in a product or service company that is similar in size to your firm. This is critical. Many CEOs will hire a candidate based on "big-company" experience. **This is a mistake**. The responsibilities and daily tasks of being a salesperson in a $500 million company are diametrically different than those in a $10 million firm or a smaller start-up.

Time and time again, I have seen candidates hired because their résumés showed big-company experience. Because sales managers and top executives aspire to big-company growth, they believe that big-company experience will transfer success to their firm.

As a guideline for hiring salespeople, take your company's current annual sales range, and then *quadruple* it. Use this number as the benchmark for hiring new account executives. For example, if your firm is a $20 million player expecting to be a $60 million player in five years, it may be difficult for a salesperson from a $200 million company to adapt to your day-to-day sales tasks. You may find a great candidate who can assimilate quickly into a small company culture, but it is unusual.

Always hire based on your firm's life cycle. Never hire someone whose current daily sales tasks are not consistent with your company's daily sales tasks.

It is not uncommon for corporate management to change 100% of the sales account managers (and sometimes their management team) every three to five years in a growing firm. As companies evolve through changing life cycles, different types of sales talent and personalities (as mentioned earlier) are needed to fit their organizational growth needs. Do not be concerned by this, as long as the transition is a slow, steady process controlled by premeditated replacement of salespeople, as the sales model dictates. Accept this as part of the criteria for your firm to be successful.

Guideline Four—Evaluate Compatibility and Stability

Determine if you can work with this person. If you are the senior hiring manager, you have to be able to manage this sales candidate. At times, firms that are revenue hungry need Cowboy personalities on their sales teams, but they have to be manageable and measurable in their skill sets or you are wasting the job requisition on the wrong candidate. As a manager interviewing candidates, remember that the candidate doesn't have to have a sales style or communication skills similar to yours. It is not uncommon for sales managers to hire people like themselves. This is a form of "Parallel Imaging." Just keep in mind—they are not you. Maybe you are a Hunter and the candidate is a Cowboy. That's okay. But, can you work with him?

At the end of the day, it is your responsibility to help the sales team reach its quota. Don't just hire a warm body because you need to fill an open position to hit your monthly revenue numbers. Hire correctly in the beginning and you will have a better chance of consistently hitting your department's sales quota targets.

Consider adding this question to your evaluation process:

> **Interview Question:** Have you been at your current job at least two years?
>
> **Correct Answer:** Yes
>
> Do not hire people who have not been at their last two jobs at least two years. The sales profession is an unstable employment environment. Hire salespeople who are more stable than the market as a whole. Salespeople who show a pattern of moving every year or eighteen months most likely have issues that you do not want on your team.

Guideline Five—Evaluate Skill Sets

Determine if the candidate's skill sets and personality match your firm's life cycle. Hiring a **Trotter** when you need a **Hunter** or a **Cowboy** will only defeat the purpose. Yes, you might run into a good candidate at the wrong time, but the key is hiring the right type to fill your needs, not filling an open job requisition with the wrong person.

Consider adding these questions to your evaluation process:

>**Interview Question:** What titles do you primarily sell to?
>
>**Correct Answer:** Directors and above
>
>Selling to management is the key to increase sales. Anyone can sell to lower-level supervisors and middle management. Getting to senior management, creating value, and communicating why prospects should buy from you versus a competitor is a specialized skill that you need to have on your sales team.
>
>**Interview Question:** Do you do your own executive presentations?
>
>**Correct Answer:** Yes
>
>Many salespeople rely on technical and operations support staff for executive presentations. Often selling products and services requires a team effort to successfully complete the sale. But, successful salespeople realize that they must be able to interact with management in a knowledgeable format. This requires them to manage and lead all

executive presentations instead of depending on team members to pick up the slack.

Guideline Six—Evaluate Current Compensation

When reviewing the candidate's current compensation, look for a maximum base salary of 50% of total compensation; and preferably 33% of total compensation. Someone who makes 75% to 90% of his total compensation from a base salary (or non-refundable draw) generally is not going to be motivated by an incentive-based program.

Why would a salesperson hunt for new sales opportunities when 75% of his income is guaranteed?

Consider adding this question to your evaluation process:

> **Interview Question:** Was at least 50% of your last W-2 from commissions?
>
> **Correct Answer:** Yes
>
> Salespeople should make a maximum of 50% of their total income in salary, preferably only 33%, and the rest in commissions and/or bonuses. Salespeople are driven by motivational incentive programs—one of which is money. When a sales candidate's current compensation is mostly salary or a nonrefundable draw, she is coming from an

employment environment that did not induce her to sell at her highest level.

Guideline Seven—Evaluate Lead Generation Methods

Always ask sales candidates how they find business leads. If they <u>do not say "cold calling,"</u> don't hire them. Today, more than ever, all sales personalities need to prospect for new business from existing customers and new prospects. When a candidate says "I network," he is actually saying you need to give me qualified leads. Networking <u>is not</u> a scalable or replicable sales process. Yes, some salespeople bring prior business contacts that create short-term revenue opportunities—but, what happens when these opportunities are used up? Simply knowing a prospect does not mean the prospect has a buying demand. Networking is a short-term model of revenue capture and results in a shallow forecast. All salespeople must include cold calling in their arsenal of tools to hit their sales quotas.

Consider adding this question to your evaluation process:

> **Interview Question:** How do you find prospects to sell?
>
> **Correct Answer:** Cold calling
>
> The candidate could say networking, cold calling, and inbound leads from marketing—

but, they must cold call. If you are trying to grow top-line revenues, you must hire salespeople who hunt for business through outbound prospect capture.

Guideline Eight—Check References

When checking references, always talk with the person who directly managed the sales candidate during the last five years of the candidate's employment. Often salespeople give sales associates or old customers as references, but this is unacceptable for reference checking.

Unfortunately, in this world of political correctness and potential lawsuits, it is hard to get accurate information on sales candidates. A great question to ask any sales manager about one of her former salespeople is "Would you hire him again?" This question allows the manager to respond either yes or no without saying why.

Additionally, when getting telephone numbers for references, only accept office numbers, not home numbers or cell phones, to prevent your candidate's friends from posing as business contacts.

Consider adding this question to your evaluation process:

> **Interview Question:** Would your current or previous employer hire you again?
>
> **Correct Answer:** Yes

This is a key question to help determine if their current management team likes the sales candidate. In this litigious world of business, references often will not say what they really believe. If an employer would hire the sales candidate again, this is a good sign. The candidate is asked this question to judge his response, and obtain references from previous jobs.

Guideline Nine—Evaluate Career Educational Investment

Determine if the sales candidate has invested in himself with ongoing training (courses, books, seminars, etc.) to increase his sales success. In a research study through our free sales strategy newsletter, **BDM News** (www.bdmnews.com), we confirmed that top quota hitting salespeople always invest in their own sales training. When salespeople don't invest, they may not take their careers seriously.

Consider adding this question to your evaluation process:

> **Interview Question:** Have you personally invested in any sales training for yourself during the last year?
>
> **Correct Answer:** Yes

Studies confirm that salespeople who purchase training books, courses, and seminars using their own money are always more successful than their peers who wait for company-provided training. Hire salespeople who see sales as a profession.

Guideline Ten—Evaluate Dedication to Your Job Offering

Never hire salespeople who have been self-employed for more than one year. When a sales candidate has worked for himself longer than a year, he is always thinking about the next entrepreneurial endeavor—on your salary.

Consider adding this question to your evaluation process:

> **Interview Question:** Have you ever owned your own business?
>
> **Correct Answer:** No
>
> Many salespeople believe their employment in sales is just a way station until they get "a real job." Being a professional salesperson is like owning your own business in many ways, because of the independence. Never hire a candidate who has worked for himself full-time for more than one year. Most salespeople try to work for themselves at least once, but most discover it is more difficult than it

appears. If a candidate's résumé indicates rolling in and out of self-employment, do not hire him because he will be planning his next business start-up on your salary.

Through our management consulting practice, we often interview senior sales candidates and VPs of Sales for management teams not as a search firm, but in the capacity as a third-party advisor. These interviews are scheduled conference calls and the management teams often listen to the interview both as a training tool for themselves and to hear first-hand the candidate's response to many of the questions.

The main rule of hiring salespeople is always hire slow . . . but terminate fast.

The Hiring Tool That Makes or Breaks a Candidate

Before you make a job offer, always have your sales candidate build a 90-day sales plan outlining how he will become educated on your business operations and policies, as well as how he will attack his assigned sales territories and prospect opportunities. This pre-employment request will help you see how the candidate thinks, how organized he is, and if he understands the process of sales. Remember, you don't want to hire the best salesperson available at the time of the opening; instead you want to hire the best salesperson.

Chapter 4
Hiring the Right Salespeople

Candidate Primary Question Interview Sheet

Candidate's Name_____

Date Interviewed_____

Interviewer_____

Questions

1. How do you find prospects to sell?
   Cold Calling _____   Other_____

2. Did you hit your quota the last 2 years or more?
   Yes_____   No_____

3. What titles do you primarily sell to?
   Director/Above_____   Other_____

4. Did you make your quota by selling to new prospects?
   Yes_____   No_____

5. Have you been at your current job at least two years?
   Yes_____   No_____

6. Do you do your own executive demos/presentations?
   Yes_____   No_____

7. Have you personally invested in any sales training for yourself during the last year?
   Yes_____   No_____

8. Was at least 50% of your last W-2 from commissions?
   Yes_____   No_____

9. Would your current employer hire you again?
   Yes_____   No_____

10. Have you ever owned your own business?
    Yes_____   No_____

Chapter 4
Hiring the Right Salespeople

Investing in Your Sales Team

The question many chief financial officers and financial managers ask of the senior sales manager is *how much and how often should you invest in salespeople to maximize your return on your assets (salespeople)*? To calculate this answer, let's look at the life cycle of an average sales rep.

Lifecycle of a Successful Sales Rep

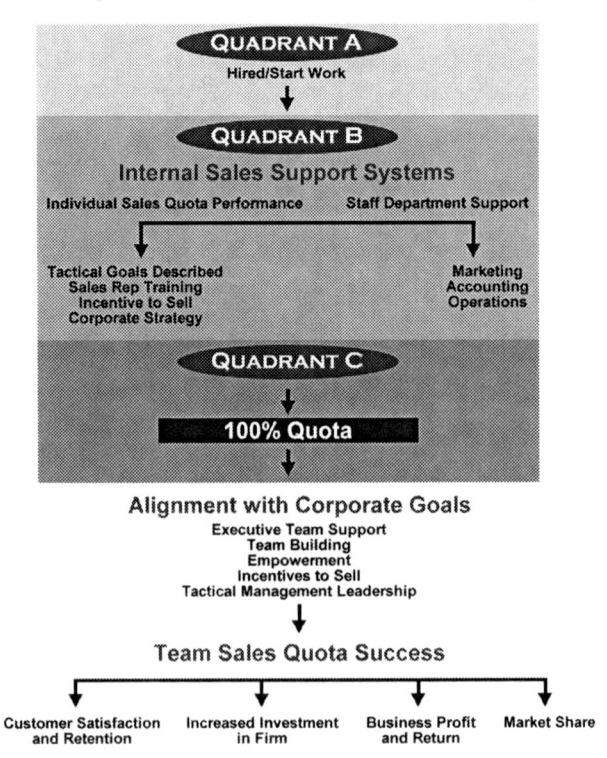

QUADRANT A
Hired/Start Work
↓
QUADRANT B
Internal Sales Support Systems

Individual Sales Quota Performance	Staff Department Support
Tactical Goals Described Sales Rep Training Incentive to Sell Corporate Strategy	Marketing Accounting Operations

QUADRANT C
↓
100% Quota
↓
Alignment with Corporate Goals
Executive Team Support
Team Building
Empowerment
Incentives to Sell
Tactical Management Leadership
↓
Team Sales Quota Success

| Customer Satisfaction and Retention | Increased Investment in Firm | Business Profit and Return | Market Share |

Source: *BDM News*

Chapter 4
Hiring the Right Salespeople

Quadrant A: The time frame of hiring and probation.

Quadrant B: The time frame for sales training, sales pipeline development, and company support.

Quadrant C: The time frame that reflects the success of a sales rep's account closing.

Most accounting departments do not equate investment in sales training as an investment in asset management, but the term *sales training* is a misnomer. In fact, the key phrase is **sales learning**.

Sales Learning ROI Graph

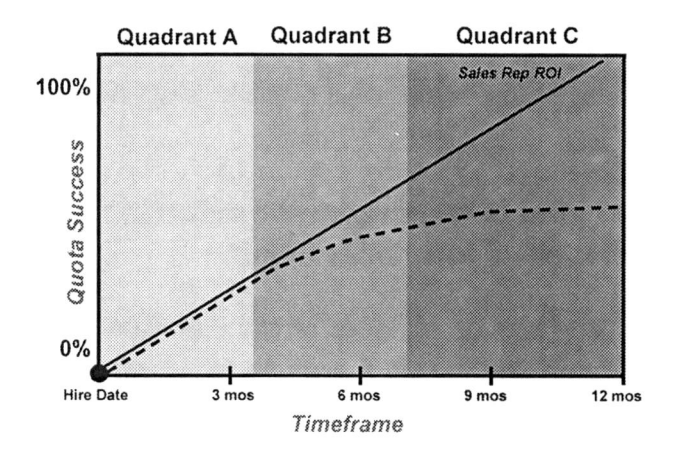

Legend:
— Sales rep's lifecycle with ongoing sales training investment.
- - - Sales rep's lifecycle without ongoing sales training investment.

Source: *BDM News*

As you can see by the **Sales Learning ROI Graph**, the greatest ROI is when you invest in ongoing training and company support in Quadrant A and B and then continue into Quadrant C. As you move further away from the actual hire date, you will see that the success and level of ROI is determined by the ongoing support provided to the sales rep. Training intermittently or at the end of a sales rep's life cycle will return the smallest of ROI.

Sales learning must be consistent or you are wasting your asset (the sales team).

Managing Cultural Performance

Matching the correct account executive with your current and future sales goals is important to the success of your sales team. However, your business culture and sales behavioral culture must match as well.

The next goal is to increase the cultural performance of your sales team!

Selling products or services to management is a premeditated sport. It is a process of planned calculated steps. When managed correctly, these steps help minimize failure and increase sales quota success.

To increase sales success, you need to balance your firm's cultural and business environment with your sales strategy implementation and sales team's needs and expectations.

Sales is not a silo process, focused on capturing revenue independently. Revenue capture is a team sport, requiring the alignment of marketing, strategy, and operations, as well as accounting, to help the sales team sell more. It is critical that the corporate business progression be aligned with the cultural progression of your team. Having a business process that ignores the cultural process will ultimately affect your company's ability to hit its revenue goals.

One way to forecast your sales team's potential success is by measuring its cultural acceptance of your management style.

Chapter 4
Hiring the Right Salespeople

Take Our Sales Cultural Audit Test

1. Are your sales account managers asked for input before they are assigned an annual sales quota?

    ____Yes   ____No

2. Has your sales team been given a written sales process on how it should sell prospects?

    ____Yes   ____No

3. Has your sales team been supplied a buyer prototype that identifies the ideal prospect it should approach and sell?

    ____Yes   ____No

4. Does your sales team receive monthly financial incentives (MBOs or management by objectives, or sales scorecard goals) to induce them into specific sales steps (cold calls, presentations, etc.)?

    ____Yes   ____No

5. Does your sales team meet at least quarterly to create a team *esprit de corps*?

    ____Yes   ____No

6. Does your sales team role-play at least once a month and evaluate each other's performances?

    ____Yes   ____No

7. Do you have a centralized information repository (i.e., employee portal, website, etc.) where sales team members can deposit or collect sales and marketing support materials and competitive information, and post requests for help from sales peers to help them close more business?

    ____Yes   ____No

Chapter 4
Hiring the Right Salespeople

8. Do you have detailed job descriptions for your sales team members (signed by the respective person), outlining management's expectations of their performance on a weekly, monthly, and annual basis?

   ____Yes   ____No

9. Does your sales team receive quarterly written performance reviews with recommendations for improvements?

   ____Yes   ____No

10. Are sales team members asked annually what their financial and career goals are?

    ____Yes   ____No

Correct Answers:

All correct answers are *yes* and each correct answer is worth 10%.

How did you score? The higher your score, the more your sales behavioral culture matches your business culture.

Sales culture is just as important as sales skills and strategy. The sales team's business expectations must match management's expectations to maximize your company's revenue capture opportunities. When a sales team's cultural environment is not aligned with management's business expectations, sales team members become disenchanted and, ultimately, low performers.

To maximize sales success, make sure your sales team has the business values and expected behavior needed for revenue success. Just a small change in your team's cultural behavior can have a dramatic effect in sales.

Establishing Sales Job Descriptions

The following are two templates for sales job descriptions: one for Hunters and one for Farmers. The primary difference between the two are Hunters cold call new prospects and Farmers cold call existing customers. Players, Cowboys and Trotters fall within the Hunter description since they are all aggressive outbound types. (You should consult with an attorney before implementing these descriptions.)

Chapter 4
Hiring the Right Salespeople

Hunter Sales Position—Job Description

Overview

This corporate sales position is a member of the sales department and is responsible for meeting or exceeding assigned sales quotas, following all corporate policies on sales, marketing, and customer service, and maintaining a positive work environment with your work associates. Your primary function is to generate business through new prospects.

Position Reports To: VP of Sales and Marketing or Sales Manager

Required Reports: Weekly sales summary submitted to the vice president of sales no later than Monday of each week for the previous week. This sales summary includes the previous week's business accomplishments, the current week's expected accomplishments, and areas needing executive direction.

Job Function and Responsibilities

- Must understand the company's current and future offerings.
- Travel to account sites as needed. All long-distance travel must be approved by the vice president of sales or sales manager. All air travel must be pre-approved by your direct manager in writing, with an estimated cost prior to booking.
- Must cold call a minimum of **25 new prospects a day** or as needed to hit your assigned new-business sales quota.
- Must understand and follow the company's operation sales policies.
- Meet or exceed monthly, quarterly, and annual assigned sales quotas as directed by the vice president of sales and the executive committee.
- When directed, must work with the accounting department in the collection of unpaid invoices.
- Communicate all prospect and client activity to the executive team.

- Submit all expense reports with expense detail within a timely manner to the accounting department.
- Document and record daily all sales prospect information into the corporate CRM/Contact system.
- Communicate product or service issues, as related by prospects and existing clients, to the vice president of engineering for adjustment and management.
- Work in parallel with the vice president of sales and the VP of Engineering to drive pilots/RFIs/RFPs to success.
- Attend and contribute in all sales meeting discussions as required.
- Provide a positive work environment for all staff.
- Abide by all corporate pricing policies.

I understand and accept my responsibilities as described in this job description.

Name_____Date_____

Corporate Witness_____Date_____

Chapter 4
Hiring the Right Salespeople

Farmer Sales Position—Job Description

Overview

This corporate sales position is a member of the sales department and is responsible for meeting or exceeding assigned sales quotas and following all corporate policies on sales, marketing, and customer service, and maintaining a positive work environment with your work associates. Your primary function is to generate business through existing customers.

Position Reports To: VP of Sales and Marketing or Sales Manager

Required Reports: Weekly sales summary submitted to the vice president of sales no later than Monday of each week for the previous week. This sales summary includes the previous week's business accomplishments, the current week's expected accomplishments, and areas needing executive direction.

Job Function and Responsibilities

- Must understand the company's current and future offerings.
- Travel to account sites as needed. All long-distance travel must be approved by the vice president of sales. All air travel must be pre-approved by your direct manager in writing, with an estimated cost prior to booking.
- Must **cold call a minimum of 25 existing customers a day** or as needed to hit your assigned existing-customer sales quota.
- Must understand and follow the company's operation sales policies.
- Meet or exceed monthly, quarterly, and annual assigned sales quotas as directed by the vice president of sales and the executive committee.
- When directed, must work with the accounting department in the collection of unpaid invoices.

Chapter 4
Hiring the Right Salespeople

- Must work with existing clients to extend long-term relationships and maximize customer lifetime value.
- Communicate all prospect and client activity to the executive team.
- Submit all expense reports with expense detail within a timely manner to the accounting department.
- Document and record daily all sales prospect information into the corporate CRM/Contact system.
- Communicate product or service issues, as related by prospects and existing clients, to the vice president of engineering for adjustment and management.
- Work in parallel with the vice president of sales and the VP of Engineering to drive pilots/RFIs/RFPs to success.
- Attend and contribute in all sales meeting discussions as required.
- Provide a positive work environment for all staff.
- Abide by all corporate pricing policies.

I understand and accept my responsibilities as described in this job description.

Name_____Date_____

Corporate Witness_____Date_____

Success Factors of Salespeople Who Hit Their Quota

During the last couple of years, DigitalHatch's free weekly sales strategy newsletter, ***BDM News***, has surveyed thousands of salespeople about their sales quotas. This survey indicated seven consistent variables of salespeople who hit their sales quotas which are:

1. They cold call.
2. They invest in their own training.
3. They sell results, not features or functions.
4. They talk like the buyer.
5. They accept that sales is their career.
6. They often role-play being a buyer or seller.
7. They plan their sales process.

When hiring salespeople, seek candidates who have these characteristics and you will increase your sales team success.

Chapter 4
Hiring the Right Salespeople

Chapter 5

Sales Team Compensation Plans

After reading this chapter, you will know:

- How to develop compensation plans that are efficient for the company, yet rewarding for salespeople

- How to implement new compensation plans to allow salespeople to "buy in" to the new program

- Why incentives can be very effective for higher performance

- What type of incentives other companies offer

Compensation for sales teams is always a political, social, and economic challenge for sales management. It is a common assumption held by most salespeople that they are overworked and underpaid. Yet, in today's economy many salespeople are often not paid based on the work ethic they commit to or the business results they produce.

Chapter 5
Sales Team Compensation

Selling, in its truest form, is a result-based employment opportunity that should pay based on success, not the anticipation of success. In the real world, since compensation inflation is rampant in many industries, sales management must learn to work with the available pool of sales candidates and modify their approach to sales to increase their potential for success. This is even more relevant today due to the fact that many companies must hire the best salesperson at the time of the open requisition and business need, not necessarily the best salesperson available in the candidate pool.

Simultaneously, when you have a salesperson who is above average in sales skills and is a team player, you should *overpay* them market value.

Let me repeat this, if you have salespeople who are exceptional, you need to pay them *more* than market value. In this market, where many average salespeople are overpaid, when you find a high achiever, it costs you more if you lose him to a competitor. (See Chapter 9 on lost sales analysis.)

Most compensation plans are made of salary, commission, and some type of sales awards.

The goal of any sales compensation is to drive specific behavior.

Developing a Compensation Plan

When your sales team is not hitting its assigned sales numbers, usually one variable that influences the lack of success is your sales compensation.

What guidelines should you use when developing a compensation plan for your salespeople?

1. Your compensation plan should be incentive-based with at least 50% of total income being variable income tied to performance and 33% of total compensation being assigned to a base as a targeted goal.

2. If you pay commissions, then the commissions should be tied (in whole or in part) to the customer's accounts receivables collection—except for business annuities like annuity sales, ASP software sales, and other types of long-term buy options.

3. Establish sales compensation plans so that 75% of your sales team can hit the sales quota number annually.

4. Develop sales compensation plans that include sales territory sharing, specific account sharing splits, and length of account ownership.

5. Make sure you do not develop annual compensation plans where salespeople can

Chapter 5
Sales Team Compensation

become highly paid account executives by maintaining existing accounts.

6. To help keep salespeople for extended periods of time, offer annual "longevity bonuses" to those salespeople who stay an additional year, and then pay the bonus over six months.

7. When negotiating with new sales candidates, and even existing sales staff, for a salary increase, think about offering a non-refundable draw or bonus against future commissions instead of a permanent base salary increase. This will reduce your total base salary raises over time.

8. Develop different sales compensation plans for EACH different sales job you have (i.e., inside sales, Hunters, Farmers, key account salespeople, etc.).

9. Use monthly financial incentive bonuses called MBOs (management by objectives) and Sales Scorecard metrics that will drive targeted performance monitored by sales metrics, like the number of cold calls per week or number of prospect presentations per month.

10. With sales cycles shorter than 90 days, pay a higher commission and a lower base salary than sales opportunities longer than 90 days.

Chapter 5
Sales Team Compensation

11. To increase success with specific targeted products, services, industries, or new markets, pay different commissions or bonuses to induce action by your sales team. For example, a $1,000 bonus for selling the "X" product or service.

12. Based on the average gross margins and gross profitability of your product or service offering, most companies offer annual sales compensation (including commissions and base salary) from 8% to 15% (fully loaded with benefits and expenses) of total sales of the salesperson.

13. Build into your sales compensation specific benefits that may be unique to the candidate (i.e., college tuition, flextime, work at home, etc.).

14. Hold quarterly sales compensation and performance reviews with your salespeople to confirm their income goal successes.

15. Always pay more in commission for sales to new prospects (Hunters) than sales to existing customers (Farmers).

16. Always have separate sales quotas for sales to new prospects and sales to existing customers.

17. When trying to determine what to pay salespeople, start with a financial number you think the job is worth at sales quota, then work backward to develop your comp plan.

18. If your team sells both products and services, have separate sales quotas for each.

These guidelines will help you develop compensation plans that are reflective of the work being provided by the salesperson.

Implementing New Sales Compensation Plans

When it comes time to implement a new compensation plan, take six months to roll out your new plan, grandfathering your old compensation plan, to allow existing salespeople to "buy in" to the new program. New hires should be subject to the new compensation plan.

Run multiple realistic product and service sales scenarios and gross margin opportunities to test the income compensation effects on your new compensation plan.

Do market research on what your industry and region pays for the same sales effort.

Meet with your sales team prior to implementing your new sales plan and describe for them the business results you are seeking (new business sales, number of cold calls per month, etc.) and ask for their input on a compensation plan that would be fair.

Manage your new sales program from the top down. If management does not handle unusual sales anomalies when they occur, the compensation plan will not drive targeted sales action steps correctly.

Pay what the job is worth. Start with a targeted compensation goal for each job position at 100% of quota and work backward to determine how you are going to fund the compensation.

Developing an Incentive Program

Salespeople, by their very nature, are competitive. They are competitive with their personal goals, their sales team's goals, and their individually assigned sales target or quota.

Some of my clients have developed some unusual and rewarding bonuses for individual sales quota success, team sales quota success, and top salesperson of the year.

Money is not everything. Yes, it does motivate, but many management teams are using different options today in an effort to stimulate their sales team to greater peak performance. In fact, many success

Chapter 5
Sales Team Compensation

awards are items that salespeople would not buy for themselves because of family commitments.

Top 10 Unusual and Financially Rich Sales Incentives Companies Offer

1. A Mercedes Benz 500 SL or Porsche 911 one-year lease for the top salesperson.

2. A free day at a spa for each salesperson who hits their monthly sales quota.

3. Two Super Bowl tickets, airline tickets and hotel suite for the top salesperson of the year.

4. A 2 week vacation for two anywhere in the world up to a $20,000 purchase price -- awarded to the top salesperson with the balance in cash.

5. A weekend for two to a Ritz Carlton Hotel -- if you hit your quarterly sales quota.

6. Choice of a 7 day white water trip vacation for two, a 7 day vacation trip to the Caribbean, or a 7 day all-expense paid trip for two to New York City including Broadway tickets, etc.

7. A 7 day all-expense paid trip for two to the Bellagio Hotel & Casino in Las Vegas in a four room suite and $5,000 spending (or gambling) money.

Chapter 5
Sales Team Compensation

8. A $100 gift certificate to different restaurants each month a salesperson hits their monthly quota.

9. A 7-foot high trophy for the salesperson of the year with a 2 week all-expense paid trip to a dude ranch for four or trip to Fiji for two.

10. Race car training at the Skip Barber Racing Car School for each salesperson who hits their quarterly sales quota.

So, how does your company's motivational incentives compare? Are you giving a handshake and a plaque at the annual company banquet?

Are some of these incentive offerings over the top?

Not necessarily. The goal of any incentive program, if developed and positioned correctly, is to drive individual and team performance to greater heights of all sales team members. Just giving more money to salespeople often does not stimulate someone to greater success because they will just take the money and pay bills or invest it and see no immediate positive reinforcement.

But providing a brand new Mercedes Benz 500 SL convertible that costs $100,000 to the top salesperson reinforces to the salespeople that if they work hard, they will receive a rare luxury item with which to enjoy their success. And to keep this badge

Chapter 5
Sales Team Compensation

of success, they need to keep working hard or they may lose the car the next year.

The costs to management for these types of incentive programs are usually incremental. You can lease the 500 SL for $2,000 a month, send someone to Vegas with gambling money for $10,000, or buy a 7-foot trophy for $500. But offering unusual performance awards that are more "demonstratively visible" teases the rest of the sales team with what they could receive if they just try a little harder.

Imagine, if your firm could increase its sales team quota performance by another 15-20% by offering these types of awards, **how much would that be worth to you?**

More than ever, the asset value of most companies is not the product or service they sell—but the strength of the company's sales distribution.

Invest in your value.

Chapter 6

Training Salespeople

After reading this chapter, you will know:

- Why sales training is essential for your team's success

- How to develop a sales training program

- What tools can be used to develop an effective sales training program

Depending on what product or service you sell, your investment in hiring a salesperson is usually a one-year commitment. By the time you hire, train, and monitor the person's sales success, you usually burn 6-8 months of your fiscal budget selling time. If you let the person go, you start the whole process over.

So, when you hire a new salesperson . . . it is a one-year commitment.

The way to maximize your investment (the sales team) is to minimize mistakes, accelerate the revenue-capture process, and reduce sales costs by thoroughly training them when they are first hired and continually training during their employment.

Chapter 6
Training Salespeople

Sales training programs are often discussed as an important business tool, but in most companies it is more talk than action. We have worked with tens of thousands of salespeople and have found that training investments increase when sales teams start missing their quotas. This reactive approach to training can be prevented by proactively investing instead of waiting for the sales team to fail.

6 Reasons Why Most Companies Do Not Give More Sales Training

1. Companies don't budget for it.

2. Companies give sales training briefly when a new salesperson is hired and assume that is enough.

3. Management believes (or their salespeople believe) they are too senior to learn anything new.

4. In general, training salespeople is a low priority for the company.

5. Companies cannot afford to have their "busy" salespeople out of their selling territories.

6. Management feels salespeople are already paid too much and should be knowledgeable about their jobs.

Guidelines for Training Your Sales Team

To increase sales success, provide more sales training. The following guidelines will help you develop a sales training program.

- **Give structured sales training for at least two weeks at the beginning of the employee's employment.** It should include how to cold call, give executive presentations, manage competition, handle sales objections, prepare proposals, negotiate contracts and sell key accounts.

- **Hold structured sales training at least two hours each month.** Training can be used as a refresher on sales techniques covered at the onset of employment, new topics to provide advanced sales skills, as well as discussion on existing deals that would help them manage their time and sales cycle more effectively.

- **Commit one full day each quarter to a structured sales training class.** Any less than this, and you risk lowering the success rate of your sales team.

Making Your Sales Training More Successful

To maximize your sales training, you should plan your training using a structured approach, rather than a reactive approach. Here are some tools to help you develop a structured sales training program.

Sales Reports. If you require your team to provide weekly sales reports that identifies items they need help with, then you have a good idea of the challenges each salesperson is encountering. Oftentimes, if one person faces a challenge, another salesperson will face that same challenge (or similar one) at another time. Sales reports are excellent sources for identifying training needs.

Have sales team members discuss at sales meetings a current prospect issue or stumbling block they are encountering and have the team give input on the next action steps to take.

Sales Objections. Collect the top sales objections heard by your sales team by prospect title you sell to (CFO, COO, vice president of marketing, etc.) and industry verticals (healthcare, insurance, etc.) Document these objections and create written responses for each.

Sales Mentors. Assign a sales mentor to each new salesperson during the first 90 days of their employment, so new salespeople can leverage the knowledge from experienced sales team members.

Industry Research. Review and discuss the top 5 business problems of the verticals you sell, based on recent industry research in trade publications.

Customer Documentation. Document and discuss why prospects buy from you, based on the business title of the buyer. Sales training should help salespeople understand why different prospect titles buy from your firm.

Role-Playing. Have each sales team member role-play at least once a week, rotating as the buyer and the seller. Role-playing is a key sales training tool that will increase their sales success. As such, I have expanded on this topic below.

Role-Playing Tips to Increase Success

Role-playing is an underused sales tool. When employed correctly, it can increase your sales team success, identify sales skill gaps, and allow you to develop an *esprit de corps* amongst your sales team as they experience sales education as a group.

Conversely, when incorrectly used, role-playing embarrasses your sales account managers, produces poor sales and management interaction, and hides sales training requirements from your executive staff.

It is estimated that only **21%** of sales teams actually role-play sales issues and objections.

So, how should role-playing be used?

Role-playing is a business tool to manage stress when communicating to prospects.

As stress increases during prospect interaction, salespeople lose control of their verbal responses, shoot from the hip, and simultaneously lose control of the sales cycle. Stress develops when salespeople are not prepared to respond to the weaves and bobs of prospect questioning. Managing prospect questioning through a trained process will reduce stress and increase sales success.

In order for your sales team to get the most out of it, sales role-playing, like any other training tool, needs to be a structured process with guidelines. The sales program should have specific goals based on written objectives. Pulling a salesperson into a corner office and grilling her as an executive buyer may be as effective as focusing on targeted sales skill improvement based on increasing efficiency on sales techniques, like prospect questioning, cold calling, product or service presentations, etc.

1. **Never make role-playing easy.**
   Salespeople must learn to be able to handle pressure (and stress) in the form of difficult inbound questions from prospects, based on the prospects' need to know about your offerings value, price, competitive

Chapter 6
Training Salespeople

positioning, and feature/function offers. Being tough in role-playing makes salespeople ready for any situation or outcome.

2. **Role-play by title of buyers.**
Salespeople need to adapt their verbal communication skills to different buyer titles. The way you sell to a CFO of a Fortune 1000 firm is diametrically different than to a president of a small private firm.

3. **Split role-playing between sales peers and sales management.**
Role-playing should be carried out by both sales management and sales team members, to allow for diversity of approach and experience. Have each sales team member take a turn being the buyer and the seller.

4. **When role-playing with salespeople, redirect all conversations away from the sales process.**
At times, prospects (even qualified prospects) will change subjects and steer salespeople away from sales cycle conversation. To sell to management, salespeople need to chitchat less and stay on the targeted goals of the conversation by qualifying the prospect and moving forward in the sales cycle. Role-play with sales team members to see how quickly and succinctly they bring back their prospect's conversation

to the discussion about relevant business issues.

5. **Record all role-playing sessions.**
Role-playing is a reusable, educational tool that should be listened to over and over again. By recording your role-playing sessions, you can later document great sales objection responses and disseminate them to your sales team.

6. **Document each salesperson's role-playing strengths and weaknesses.**
Role-playing is a replicable, scalable sales tool. Understanding and managing your team members' skill sets will help them hit sales quotas faster. If a salesperson crumbles under the pressure of role-playing with his peers or his direct sales manager, how will he perform with a prospect? How many qualified prospects is he losing by saying the wrong thing? Through role-playing, you can help individual salespeople increase their sales quota success.

7. **Make a list of your top ten sales objections and use them during your role-playing sessions.**
Selling to management is just managing their understanding of your product or service value. Value is communicated based on your ability to show the prospect how you can help fix their business pain. Always

Chapter 6
Training Salespeople

role-play your 10 toughest sales objections so salespeople can learn how to manage value expectations when confronted with the most common objections and questions.

To sell more—role-play more!

Chapter 6
Training Salespeople

Chapter 7

Managing Your Sales Team

After reading this chapter, you will know:

- How to manage salespeople who work in virtual offices

- How to prepare for a ride-along

- How to get the most out of a ride-along for yourself and the salesperson

Managing Salespeople Who Work in Virtual Offices

Today, many companies use virtual offices to reduce sales costs. But virtual offices expose management to abuses and lower sales team productivity if not managed correctly. To manage virtual offices more effectively, implement the following:

1. Review all phone bills monthly to determine work start times and end times of your salespeople. If you see only 7 outbound sales calls a day that start at 10:00 a.m. and end at 11:00 a.m., it may be a sign that you have a salesperson who has a good golf game.

2. Manage all virtual sales offices by weekly metric reports. For example, how many cold calls per week, how many out-of-office appointments, etc.

3. Make all salespeople who work in a virtual office sign a contract that says they will not operate a business (directly or indirectly by themselves, or through another family member or colleague) while they are employed by you. Many salespeople dream about working for themselves and think it's a good idea to start their new venture while on your payroll. You should include a clause in their employment papers that requires them to reimburse your firm 100% of all salary, commissions, and expenses from the time they started marketing their new (or existing) business while they were employed by you. (Consult with your attorney or your legal department to implement this.)

4. Establish a sense of *esprit de corps* with your team by holding mandatory weekly conference calls with all salespeople who work virtually.

5. Try to hold a monthly regional meeting in the office for all salespeople to extend their camaraderie.

These recommendations will help you effectively manage salespeople who work in virtual offices.

Managing the Salesperson Ride-Along

Supervising sales teams of all sizes requires sales managers to interact with their team members on a one-to-one basis. This management interaction is implemented through various hands-on and staff engagements, depending on your title, the geographic locations of your sales team, and the type of products or services you sell.

The salesperson ride-along is a common management tool used by sales managers worldwide. A ride-along may be based on visiting current client sites, attending a new prospect opportunity, or helping negotiate or close a major deal with your account executive.

There are three variables you should consider to increase your ride-along success:

1. Understand that it is stressful for sales executives to have their sales manager around, even if they do not voice it.

2. Prior to meeting with your sales team member, send an agenda for the ride-along day listing who you are going to meet with and the business particulars (title, company name, business issues or opportunities, what you're going to sell, etc.).

3. Always meet with your sales team member first. Do not just jump in the car and head to your first appointment.

Depending on the circumstances and the client opportunities, a sales ride-along can help close more deals, educate sales staff on how to sell better, and motivate a sales team.

Conversely, if a ride-along is handled incorrectly, you can lose a deal, alienate your sales staff, and make yourself look foolish.

To be honest, most salespeople don't want their boss on a ride-along.

Salespeople believe sales managers sometimes develop executive amnesia. We have all ridden with a sales manager who said the wrong thing during a prospect meeting and caused the deal to be lost. Then later, during a review of sales call conversations, the boss forgets what he said, but reminds you of the lost revenue.

So, as a sales manager, you must create a balance between being helpful and annoying on a sales call. To increase your ride-along appointment success and your communication with the sales team, you must decide which business role (or roles) you are going to play and when.

Chapter 7
Managing Your Sales Team

- Be a mentor or sales coach to your sales team before you meet prospects or clients, and give them input of what to do in the meeting.

- Be an active sales manager when you are with prospects and clients and interject during the meeting with points you think are relevant.

- Be an invisible sales manager when you are with prospects and clients and let your sales staff handle the sales call from beginning to end by himself.

- Be a sales manager and sales coach after the appointment by advising your sales team member how the appointment went and what you might have done differently.

Each one of these options has a cause and effect impact on how your ride-along will go, but it will be helpful for your sales team member.

Is your ride-along to win business?

Are you trying to evaluate a new salesperson?

Are you trying to mentor a new sales staff member to greater performance?

You must decide before you set up a ride-along what the goals are of your meeting. Then you must align the goals with how you act. Often when doing a ride-along, you will take a hybrid approach of these four business roles. Just remember—set your goal for this meeting and work with your salesperson.

Chapter 7
Managing Your Sales Team

Ride-Along Form

Account Manager's Name_____

Ride-Along Date_____

<u>Appointment Information</u>

Account Name_____

Client Location_____

Appointment Time_____

Key Contacts to Meet:

Name_____Title_____

Name_____Title_____

Name_____Title_____

Name_____Title_____

Type of Meeting (Circle as many as needed):

  Customer Service   New Prospect Opportunity   Existing Customer   Other

What product or service has the client bought or is interested in buying?
_____

Why will you win the business?
_____

Why will you lose the business?
_____

How do you create value for the prospect?
_____

As a sales manager, how should you respond during the meeting?
_____
_____

Chapter 7
Managing Your Sales Team

Wrapping Up The Ride-Along

Ride-alongs are unique opportunities for sales managers to analyze sales rep skills, train salespeople, sell more business, and create a positive work environment. Below are four action steps to wrap up the ride-along:

1. Discuss how you felt the day went and the next sales steps needed.

2. Ask the sales executive for his input on the day's events and suggestions for improvement.

3. Always leave the ride-along on an upbeat note, even if the day was not successful.

4. Send an e-mail to the sales executive after you leave, reconfirming the topics of your wrap-up conversations and any action steps you expect the sales executive to take based on your meeting.

Use them correctly and your corporate sales will increase. They can be mutually respectful and educational for both sales management and team members.

Chapter 7
Managing Your Sales Team

Chapter 8

Holding Sales Meetings

After reading this chapter, you will know:

- How to hold group and individual meetings

- What action plans are and why they are powerful tools

- What topics can be beneficial for monthly team meetings

Sales meetings are a sales management power tool to help you increase your team's selling success and company performance. Like other management tools, its implementation approach is a key driver to it being a productive program.

Holding Team Meetings

Team meetings build camaraderie as well as competitiveness. Meetings should not be limited to just reporting weekly or monthly performance, but also provide guidance on current deals, and positive reinforcement for hard work performed. Use the following guideline to hold successful team meetings.

1. Hold a sales meeting once a week, in person or by phone.

2. Have a stated time length for each meeting, before you hold it.

3. Submit an agenda ahead of time (review your sales accounts, discuss new comp plan, etc.).

4. Start on time, end on time, and never let it last longer than one hour.

5. Have fun–don't be boring.

6. Focus on team selling issues–not the political or operational issues you have as a manager.

7. Start the meeting by complimenting one salesperson on a sales success.

8. Interact with your sales team–do not lecture your sales team. Talk to them as professionals.

9. Share information by way of explanation. Don't share information by way of instruction.

Chapter 8
Holding Sales Meetings

10. Explain at least one new sales technique at each meeting using storytelling as a tool.

11. If you are meeting in person, always hand out food or snacks to engage your team. Feed them and they will listen.

12. End your sales meeting on a positive note. Discuss a sales team success.

13. If there is an individual sales issue with one team member, discuss it outside of the meeting in a private conversation.

14. Send an e-mail to the sales team recapping the discussion points of the meeting.

Holding One-on-One Meetings

Meeting with your team members individually is a managerial requirement. These meetings happen in response to training needs, employee reviews, customer issues, prospect negotiation preparation, or just team bonding. They give you unlimited opportunities to build a productive business rapport.

Use the following outline as a guide to help you develop successful one-on-ones.

1. Pick a neutral location for all one-on-one meetings with your sales team members. Places like coffee shops, restaurants, and non-office locations help reduce stress for

both of you and creates an open environment for communication.

2. Always have a written agenda submitted to the salesperson before you meet, and stick to it. This allows the salesperson to be prepared for your discussion items, helps keep the meeting on schedule, and prevents the possibility of having your one-on-one time becoming a complaint hour.

3. Be careful about your body language. Sit straight and look at the salesperson when you speak to her, especially when reviewing difficult subjects.

4. When discussing serious or touchy subject matter (reviews, sales performance, etc.) always speak from facts, not emotion.

5. When receiving input from your salesperson that appears to be different than what you know, take written notes and don't immediately agree or disagree.

6. During the meeting, always ask the salesperson what her personal goals are (sales, income, management, etc.).

7. Once you get the salesperson to relate her goals, compare the goals to her performance, and then use this as discussion points.

Chapter 8
Holding Sales Meetings

8. In every meeting, even when giving a bad performance review, always end on a positive note.

9. Once you have finished with the one-on-one, follow up the conversation with an e-mail confirming the points you made and the action steps, if any, to be taken by you and/or the salesperson.

Developing Weekly/Monthly Manager Action Plans

Action plans are important elements to help your performance as a manager. They provide structure for both you and your team.

Weekly Action Plan

1. Hold a one-hour sales meeting with your staff.

    - Discuss sales team performance metrics as a group.

    - Discuss sales performance metrics for each salesperson.

    - Discuss the size of the team's sales forecast.

    - Give a sales training tip.

- Have one salesperson discuss a current sales situation with the group and ask for input of observations.

- Have each salesperson submit a one-page "weekly review" document that includes tasks completed last week, tasks to be completed this week, and tasks that need management help on.

2. Review all sales team forecasts for accuracy. Recommend changes to each salesperson as needed.

3. Counsel all salespeople who are below 70% year-to-date sales quotas.

4. Have one ride-along with each salesperson.

5. Review the top 20 accounts in your sales territory with assigned salespeople (status and action steps needed).

6. Submit your adjusted sales forecasts to management.

Monthly Action Plan

1. Hold a sales training session with your sales team that lasts anywhere from two hours to a full day.

2. Hold a half-hour conference call with each salesperson to discuss sales momentum and sales success in his territory.

3. Send via e-mail the team's sales success and sales metric performance to each team member.

4. Select one salesperson and name her salesperson of the month and announce it to the team.

5. Recap the top 20 sales prospects for the team and discuss sales momentum and action steps required.

As salespeople adapt to this routine, they will know what to expect. If they are experiencing problems with a deal, they are more likely to contact you proactively, rather than wait to bring it out at the sales meeting in front of the group. Additionally, salespeople by their very nature are competitive and want to be recognized for their successes. Knowing that top performers will be recognized is incentive to push themselves a little harder.

Weekly Sales Activities Report

Weekly salesperson reporting is important to link daily activities with central corporate knowledge. If the reporting is too lengthy, salespeople will not respond. Here is an example of a short 5-minute report all salespeople should use to document sales activities.

Weekly Sales Activities Report

Sales Rep Name: John Doe   **Week Ending:** May 31, 2006

Actions Completed Last Week

- Cold called 50 new prospects

- Had three on-site appointments with prospects

- Finished the Smith Proposal and hand delivered it

- Followed up on customer service issues with the Jones Company

Actions To Be Completed This Week

- Cold call 60 new prospects

- Meet with Smith again to negotiate proposal

- Two on-site meetings with prospects

- Mail direct sales letters to 100 prospects

Areas I Need Help In Or Management Involvement

- Currently need help with the ADL account on customer service issues

---

This sales management tool is a quick overview submitted to you by your sales team outlining their pre-week and post-week activities. You should have each rep send you the report once a week by e-mail in bullet format listing the activities and requests for help.

Topics for Your Monthly Sales Meetings

Coming up with topics for meetings can be challenging at times. Here are 12 topics you can use for your monthly meetings. Because products, services, industries, and your team members are constantly changing, these topics can be repeated year after year and your team will gain something new from the discussions each year.

1. How to Communicate Your Product or Service Value

2. How to Manage Price Sales Objections by Prospect Title

3. How to Present Yourself as a Business Specialist, Not a Business Generalist

4. How to Qualify Prospects–What Questions to Ask and When

5. How to Talk With Prospects So They See You as an Advisor

6. How to Understand Prospects' Business Needs and Business Pains

7. How to Manage Your Sales Time More Productively

Chapter 8
Holding Sales Meetings

8. How to Manage Prospects Who Postpone Buying Decisions

9. How to Submit a Proposal and Negotiate With Prospects

10. How to Develop an Accurate Sales Forecast

11. How to Cold Call and Create New Appointments

12. How to Network and Create Prospects

Chapter 9

Determining Sales Quotas

After reading this chapter, you will know:

- What are the top 10 most common methods used to miscalculate sales quotas

- How to accurately calculate sales quotas

- What metrics and research are needed to calculate accurate sales quotas

- How to determine territory effectiveness

- What lost sales analysis is

- Why lost sales analysis is a critical management tool

- How to determine sales effectiveness and why it is often a better indicator of sales success than just hitting a sales quota

Common Quota Calculation Mistakes

Often sales quotas are calculated based on some arbitrary corporate goal for revenue enlargement, rather than on business metrics.

Chapter 9
Determining Sales Quotas

For example, one client I consulted with was a mid-sized company where the vice president of operations and the CFO determined the sales quotas for the sales force. The vice president of operations calculated his department's overhead and then added a 40% gross margin to that number and this became the sales department's annual goal. He then took this number and divided it by the number of salespeople he thought they needed.

Voila! Like magic, they had a sales quota for the sales team.

This impractical and unscientific sales quota determination happens time and time again. More times than not, the sales quota number is based on commitments to investors, family owners, bankers, stockholders, or just aggressive business goals, combined with the accounting department's perception of what the cost of sales should be.

The short-term losers are the sales reps as they struggle to make their monthly numbers.

The long-term losers are the company's affiliated departments because they have built their business models based on this fabricated sales quota.

Here are the top ten most common methods firms use to *miscalculate* their sales quotas:

1. An increase percentage-wise over last year's territory sales numbers

Chapter 9
Determining Sales Quotas

2. The cost of the salesperson times a multiplier (salesperson's cost x 3)

3. The cost of corporate General and Administrative (G&A) overhead plus an arbitrary gross margin added in

4. Total company revenue goals committed to Wall Street or investors divided by the number of salespeople in the company

5. The total revenue goal of the vice president of sales divided by the number of salespeople available

6. A sales quota designed to support an imaginary compensation plan that was sold to the salesperson as his income potential if he hit 100% quota

7. What an industry's trade press says is the annual growth rate this year for your market (growth up 12%, quotas are up 12%)

8. The vice president of sales' quota experiences at other companies

9. A salesperson's success from the previous year in her territory (quota is 110% of last year's sales)

10. A percentage of what the top salesperson did last year in her territory (90% of what the top salesperson sold last year)

Chapter 9
Determining Sales Quotas

Are any of these methods used by your firm to calculate sales quotas?

How do these sales quota calculation methods support the potential of a particular salesperson's territory? These measurements are based on outside influences and expenses, which are completely unrelated to the sales and market potential of the product or service in an assigned territory and the ability of a salesperson to hit it.

The fact is, none of these methods are accurate.

These impractical and unscientific sales quota determination methods just frustrate everyone. When they are wrong, they affect the whole company. The operations or engineering department becomes frustrated because its capacity usage is low and they end up blaming the sales department because they haven't hit their numbers. The accounting department becomes frustrated because accounts receivables are shrinking, and investors are frustrated because their financial milestones are missed.

Are these elements important in determining your company's costs and revenue opportunities? Yes, of course; but if the approach for sales quota (or target) is backwards, then the poor results it gets should be expected.

Calculating Sales Quotas

To forecast sales goals correctly, don't determine what sales should do based on company needs. Determine what the sales department <u>can do based on the market opportunity and the sales model success your firm uses</u>. From that calculation, you can determine what other departments' overhead should be, as well as corporate G&A, to build your sales forecast.

Below is a more accurate (and simplified) sales quota determination method:

- First, determine what the true sales potential is for your product or service from each salesperson's territory, city by city and industry by industry. Determine the potential dollar size for one year of sales within the market segment or geography in which your product or service salespeople are assigned. This market potential is the *total sales potential*, not just what you can sell. Quotas do not have to be equal by sales account representative or by territory. Your marketing department should provide this information to you, or you need to calculate this yourself.

- Then, look at the length of time in months it takes for a sales lead to be generated and the number of leads needed to generate one prospect proposal. You will need sales metrics in order to determine this. If you don't have metrics in place, start collecting them. (See Chapter 11 for Sales Metrics.)

- Next, look at the average value in dollars of each product or service you sell.

- Then, determine what the average closing ratio is for all salespeople for each product and service you sell. This figure is based on number of deals proposed versus number of deals actually closed. For example, if a salesperson closes 1 out of every 4 deals, then his closing ratio is 25%.

- Last, determine the number of potential prospect leads needed to generate one qualified proposal.

With this data, you can now determine what each salesperson's target quota should be.

Now, let's use this simple formula to calculate an example quota.

Sales Quota Example:

Sales Quota = Territory potential (÷) average sale in dollars (÷) number of leads needed to generate a proposal (x) average closing ratio (x) average value of one deal.

Chapter 9
Determining Sales Quotas

Facts and Stats

Territory potential $10,000,000
Average sales value $300,000

Calculation
Territory potential divided by average sale in dollars equals potential number of sales in units.

$10,000,000 ÷ $300,000 = 33.3 sales lead potential in the territory

Facts and Stats

Number of potential unit sales in the territory 33.3
Number of leads needed to generate one proposal 4

Calculation (continued)
Number of territory potential unit sales divided by the number of leads needed to generate a proposal equals the number of potential deals per year.
33.3 ÷ 4 = 8.325 potential deals this year in this territory

Facts and Stats

Number of potential deals 8.325
Average company closing ratio
for this product or service 25%

Calculation (continued)
Number of potential deals multiplied by closing ratio equals number of actual deals sold in a territory per year.
8.325 x 25% = 2.08 deals sold in territory

Chapter 9
Determining Sales Quotas

Facts and Stats
Actual deals sold per year 2.08
Average dollar value per deal $300,000

Calculation (continued)
Number of actual deals multiplied by the average value per deal equals the annual sales quota.
2.08 x $300,000 = $624,000

Summary of Facts and Stats
Territory Potential $10,000,000
Average dollar value per deal $300,000
Number of potential unit sales in the territory 33.3
Number of leads needed to generate one proposal 4
Number of potential deals 8.325
Average company closing ratio 25%
Actual deals sold per year 2.08
Actual quota dollars per year $624,000
Average time to close a deal .... 6 months

Using this sales quota formula, you are going to find that many sales quotas are inflated and not based on actual potential or reality.

Is this a simplistic formula? *Yes.*

Does it take into consideration add-on sales for existing clients, new product introductions, or one-time large sales anomalies? *No.*

Chapter 9
Determining Sales Quotas

Can these numbers be improved by adjusting the closing ratios or the leads-to-proposal success factor? *Yes.*

These are key factors that can increase a sales rep's success and quota assignments without adjusting market size. From this sales quota calculation, you now have a benchmark that can be backed into operational delivery costs, salesperson compensation, and G&A costs to determine the corporate financial needs and revenue goals.

Does this take work? *Yes.*

Can you do it for a national sales force with 200+ account sales reps? *Absolutely.*

It is difficult to understand why so many firms generate sales forecasts based on incorrect variables and then carry the miscalculations forward. It is better to have your marketing department spend three months determining the real potential of each sales rep's territory than to guess and have all corporate budgets wrong.

As a sales manager, you need to maximize your ability to increase revenue. Increased revenue is centered on the ability to improve closing ratios, increase lead generation, maximize human capital capabilities, and forecast correctly. An accurate sales quota is the first step to managing the sales team's success.

Chapter 9
Determining Sales Quotas

Understanding Lost Sales Analysis

When managing salespeople, it is essential to understand what makes salespeople succeed or fail. One of the most successful elements of sales evaluations is a critical management tool called **"Lost Sales Analysis."**

This concept was introduced to me many years ago by a senior vice president of operations for one of the largest retail companies in the world. It made so much sense, I adopted it into my sales management methods for all sales team members regardless of the product or service being sold.

When a retail department store opens up a new location, they calculate the forecasted annual sales goal for that store based on multiple elements. These elements include traffic flow, local market demographics within a five-mile radius, the parking lot size (which affects how big the heating and air, or HVAC, system will be), and the store sales average per square foot in comparison to other similar units in the chain.

For example, let's assume that Store A has a forecasted annual sales goal of $10,000,000 per year. The senior vice president of operations noticed this did not truly reflect the store's capacity or the manager's effectiveness to produce revenue. All it did was measure the manager's ability to hit some predefined corporate goal. Based on this example, if

Chapter 9
Determining Sales Quotas

the store manager of that unit hits $11,000,000 in retail sales, or 110% of his corporate goal, he would be perceived as a high performer in most companies.

But, the senior vice president of operations wondered if this was correct.

Conversely, if a professional salesperson hits 110% of the annual quota she has been assigned, is she successful?

Would a sales rep be considered successful if she only reached 40% of quota year-to-date in the 4th Quarter, then closed one big deal that launched her to 150% of her annual quota?

The observation by this senior vice president of operations was that this measurement was an **incomplete,** arbitrary method <u>with which management had become comfortable</u>. In fact, it allowed under-performers to succeed in spite of their effort. Additionally, it penalized high performers who *did not* make their goals because of how this numerical standard measured them.

The senior vice president of operations reasoned that his company needed to add a new dimension to its business sales forecast by unit equation. They needed to factor in the total potential revenue per geography, including the competitive element revenue opportunities, to determine the unit manager's percentage of total business won and **total business lost.** He would then take the total business lost and back it into a predetermined percentage of the general manager's evaluation score to more correctly evaluate his performance and sales quota assignment.

Once they implemented this program, the retail chain immediately observed that many of the managers who had hit their annual sales quota of 100% or higher actually were under-performing **based on the potential of their regions.**

This method is much like how the car industry tracks and determines effectiveness of dealerships based on the *available market share* versus the *captured market share* within a regional area.

In most product and service markets, like the car, software and freight industries, when a sale is lost, it also means the potential recurring revenue stream is lost for three to five years (i.e., car maintenance, reorders, repairs, etc.). So, if a salesperson loses a deal in his territory, it is not just the immediate revenue lost, but generally all of the recurring revenue that would be generated by that customer through additional sales.

To focus only on sales sold as a percentage of quota when measuring success, underestimates the firm's potential revenue within a territory and overstates a salesperson's success.

From an integrated-sales-quota-calculation approach, you do not want to focus *only* on individual sales success, but also at revenue from a territory potential as a measurement for individuals and companies.

What has happened is that many management executives have arbitrarily set up standards of measurement that have nothing to do with sales potential.

The Lost Sales Analysis method made so much sense to me, that since then, I have used this model in my consulting practice as a way to determine an individual salesperson's effectiveness coupled with his sales quota success.

Calculating Lost Sales Analysis & Sales Effectiveness

This section deals with several calculations that are important in determining how effective salespeople are in penetrating their territories.

First, let's start with some of the data you used to calculate the sales quota—territory potential, sales quota, and closing ratio.

The first calculation reflects *territory effectiveness*.

> Total sales closed ($) ÷ Territory potential ($) = Territory effectiveness (%)

Next, we'll look at *overall salesperson effectiveness*. To calculate the overall sales effectiveness, combine the salesperson's closing ratio from proposals submitted with his territory effectiveness.

> Closing ratio (%) + Territory effectiveness (%) = Overall salesperson effectiveness (%)

Lastly, we'll look at what the sales rep left behind, or the *territory availability*.

> Territory potential ($) − Proposals submitted ($) = Territory availability ($)

Example One:

Let's say the unique territory sales potential for your product or service for one account manager the first year is $10,000,000 and the sales rep's quota for the first year is $1,500,000. By dividing his quota into the territory potential, you will see that the territory effectiveness within the territory is 15%.

> $1,500,000 ÷ $10,000,000 = 15% territory effectiveness

Next, let's say the sales rep has a closing ratio of 25% from proposals submitted. Let's also say the rep hit his $1,500,000 quota.

> **25% closing ratio + 15% territory effectiveness = 40% overall salesperson effectiveness**

With a 25% closing ratio, this rep submitted $6,000,000 in proposals, thereby leaving 40% of the territory available.

> $10,000,000 − $6,000,000 = $4,000,000 (or 40%) territory available

Chapter 9
Determining Sales Quotas

So, is the rep who hits 100% of his sales quota successful?

By this equation, the salesperson was successful in hitting his sales quota and sold $1,500,000 out of a potential $10,000,000 in his market, but he only had 15% territory effectiveness within his assigned territory.

Let's look at this another way. The sales rep may have sold $1,500,000, but <u>LOST $8,500,000</u> in his territory by either not calling on prospects or not correctly communicating value to prospects successfully, thereby enabling competitors to take the business.

Since it is always easier to sell to existing customers than to new prospects, if the lost clients had a cumulative effect of recurring business opportunities of 35% per year (through new sales to the same customer, upgrades, reorders, or new service engagements), then that 100% of quota salesperson has actually cost your firm $17,425,000 or more in lost revenue over three years. ($8,500,000 x 35% x 3 + $8,500,000 = $17,425,000)

Yet, under most sales quota systems, this sales rep would be deemed successful and the senior management would just try to improve their closing ratio as the only mechanism to increase corporate revenue.

Chapter 9
Determining Sales Quotas

Example Two:

Let's say a second sales rep's territory potential is $7,000,000 per year, and her sales quota is also $1,500,000 per year.

$1,500,000 ÷ $7,000,000 = 21% territory effectiveness

Let's say the sales rep also has a closing ratio of 25% and she hits 90% of her $1,500,000 quota, or $1,350,000 (19% territory effectiveness).

25% + 19% = 44% overall salesperson effectiveness

With a 25% closing ratio, this rep submitted $5,400,000 in proposals, thereby leaving only 23% of the market available.

$7,000,000 − $5,400,000 = $1,600,000 (or 23%) market available

Although the second sales rep in Example Two achieved a lower percentage of quota sales success (90%), she is <u>more successful</u> in penetrating her territory by having an overall effectiveness of 44%.

This method of back door analysis helps sales management understand the relationships between sales, sales quota, salesmanship, territories, and lost sales opportunities. It allows executives to adjust compensation (and sales quotas) to better reflect those sales account managers who are "territory productive" and those reps who are "sales quota productive."

Remember, most sales quotas are arbitrary and do not truly reflect the actual sales success of an individual.

Chapter 9
Determining Sales Quotas

One way to improve sales success is to integrate sales quota assignment *with* territory effectiveness. By integrating these two areas, you maximize the sales potential of the assigned salesperson through balancing the relationship of territory opportunity and individual salesperson skill sets.

Generally, shooting for a territory effectiveness of **50%** or better is a good sales management goal. This way, sales reps must increase their closing ratio and their territory penetration simultaneously to meet their corporate sales goals. This will also help determine what an accurate sales quota should be territory by territory.

Resources for Market Research

Although your marketing department is responsible for calculating the market potential of your company's product or service, below is a list of companies that are aggregators of market data. It may be helpful for you to visit their websites:

- www.marketresearch.com
- www.bizminer.com
- www.findsvp.com
- www.infousa.com
- www.forrester.com

- www.researchandmarkets.com
- www.firstresearch.com

19 Factors That Affect a Salesperson's Performance

Although there are many factors that can influence whether a salesperson hits her sales quota, I have found there are 19 consistent factors that appear regularly.

Sales Skills Affecting Sales Quota Success

1. The salesperson's lack of personal initiative.
2. The salesperson's poor understanding of the client's business needs.
3. The salesperson's inability to discuss their product or service offering in detail.
4. Minimal cold call efforts by the salesperson.
5. The salesperson's lack of presentation skills.
6. The salesperson's lack of prospect negotiation skills.
7. The salesperson's inability to read sales cycle signs with the prospect.
8. Poor time management by the salesperson.

Chapter 9
Determining Sales Quotas

Management Skills Affecting Sales Quota Success

9. Poor sales management advice on account sales techniques.

10. Lack of positive motivational advice to the salesperson.

11. Management interference in account sales relationships.

12. Lack of product or service training supplied on a regular basis.

13. Lack of sales training supplied on a regular basis.

14. Incorrect sales quota calculation.

Company Issues Affecting Sales Quota Success

15. The product or service offering is not competitive.

16. The company has poor customer service.

17. The market demand for the product or service is decreasing.

18. The product or service does not work as marketed.

19. The compensation plan is incorrect.

Chapter 9
Determining Sales Quotas

Eighteen of these factors can be controlled through corporate training, market research, and adjustments to the sales process. It is only the first one—personal initiative—that is outside the control of the company.

Chapter 10

Managing Forecasts

After reading this chapter, you will know:

- What salespeople often do to manipulate your perception of how busy they are

- How to differentiate between a sales forecast and a sales pipeline

- What questions to ask your salespeople to qualify a deal to be placed in a forecast

- How to set up and tighten a sales forecast

Controlling "Sales Forecasting Moles"

Sales forecasting by its very nature is an unscientific art. The decision cycles, budgets, and purchasing needs of prospects constantly change. Sales forecasts are just snapshots of time captured on a specific time line.

All companies suffer the same paradox:

Often, the buying cycle and the selling cycle are not the same.

To thwart this issue, salespeople have become "Sales Forecasting Moles" who bury themselves (like moles) deep into their forecasts, moving prospect opportunities around month to month, trying to fill up their forecasts so they look busy to their sales managers.

Forced by low sales, inaccurate sales quotas, and senior management executives that publicly over-commit on revenue projections, they just hibernate inside their sales forecast projections by moving prospects around to look like they are accelerating the sales cycle activity. As a result, salespeople spend more time selling management than selling to prospects.

The introduction of Customer Relationship Management (CRM) and contact management programs in some ways have often made sales projections less accurate today and less able to help management teams correctly forecast sales revenues, corporate cash flow, operations needs, and production requirements.

Why would the use of CRM systems cause a decrease in accuracy when compared to manual sales forecasting tracking systems?

The reason is that CRM systems provide unfiltered data.

Prior to the widespread usage of CRM systems, sales managers massaged all sales forecasts that were

Chapter 10
Managing Forecasts

provided by their sales team *before* the information was passed on to the next level of management. This massaging allowed each level of sales management to adjust the forecasts based on the local knowledge of the individual sales reps and their optimistic approach to sales revenue capture.

Once massaged and adjusted (usually downward), the data was passed on to the next level of management for review and further adjustment.

By the time it was finally submitted for corporate acceptance, the numerical values had been adjusted to reflect a more accurate forecast based on the human element of each salesperson's capabilities, rather than a mathematical calculation based on the individual forecasting algorithm, or worse the unadjusted hopes of struggling salespeople.

This current, ineffective model coupled with open visibility and unlimited timely access of CRM forecasts by multiple layers of company management and investors, continues to communicate the wrong data on an ongoing basis. As such, most sales forecasts are not accurate reflections of true revenue opportunities, but are mirror images of sales projections verbalized as expected business milestones.

Salespeople clearly understand that management needs more data from them on current and future sales. Many individuals manipulate their data to reflect public revenue declarations or internal

Chapter 10
Managing Forecasts

expectations, and as a result, **spend a disproportionate amount of time selling management on their sales activity rather than selling to prospects.**

In fact, as sales slow, the line of demarcation of a sales *forecast* and a sales *pipeline* seem to blur. Sales reps just move prospects back and forth through this sales funnel to create visual images of sales activity for management.

Sales pipelines are imaginary events that reflect unproven opportunities. Sales forecasts are commitments to revenue by your sales team.

Yes, some firms use mathematical algorithms based on individual forecasting and closing ratios to calculate actual sales forecasts accuracies, but this also causes an imbalance in the forecasts.

Why?

Every sale, like every salesperson, has its own transactional nuances during the sales cycle. The use of "smoothed," moving statistical averages still does not always allow for the ebb and flow of a sale. Mean averages work better with sales pipelines than with sales forecasts. Have you ever noticed how your salespeople fill up their sales forecasts with the minimum amount of expected dollars communicated to them by management as minimum requirements?

Chapter 10
Managing Forecasts

So, how does sales management stop Sales Forecasting Moles?

To increase your sales forecasting accuracy, follow these guidelines:

1. Start with a sales quota that is accurate.

2. <u>Do not allow</u> general access to the CRM system by all levels of senior management or by investors. Have these individuals receive only scrubbed data given to them by the sales management team when they are ready.

3. Allow your sales management team to function as they should—as sales managers. Let them scrub the data of their direct sales subordinates before the data is submitted.

4. Don't expect your salespeople to spend a disproportionate amount of the daily sales time updating their contact management and CRM systems. They won't do it, or worse, they will just fill the CRM system with worthless data.

5. Insert into the salesperson job description, the requirement to document all prospect information into your company's CRM or contact manager daily.

6. ***Only* allow deals that can be closed within 90 days to be included in your sales forecasts.** All other opportunities should be

Chapter 10
Managing Forecasts

moved to the *sales pipeline*. This will force your sales team to quickly identify true sales prospects that can be closed immediately and will minimize all sales mole activities.

A common method used by many firms is to use their average closing time line as the length of their sales forecasts. Remember, this model gives inaccurate data because it becomes a group average.

Now, when you use this method of 90 days or less for sales forecasts, many salespeople will say it makes no sense because the product or service you offer takes at least four to ten months to sell. But, product and service sales that have long sales cycles change on a monthly basis. Business deals that are inserted into a sales pipeline often fall into a sales forecast based on changing issues. When salespeople say their average sales cycle is always longer than 90 days, what they really mean is that they don't cold call. When your salespeople cold call, they fall into your competition's sales cycle. If they fall into a prospect's buying opportunity already underway, let's say in the sixth month of a nine-month buying cycle, your salesperson's sales cycle will be three months.

So, don't let salespeople manipulate your sales forecasting model to make their sales activity look more accurate than it really is.

By implementing these guidelines, you will reduce the risk of salespeople becoming forecasting moles.

Chapter 10
Managing Forecasts

Creating a Sales Forecast

Sales forecasting is part art, part human perception, and part sales management metrics.

Salespeople need to find prospects that will take action steps with them during the sales cycle to prove they should continue to work with them. This method of sales is called **transactional selling**. Most of the time, salespeople talk about relationship selling and insert their "relationships" into the sales forecasts without any business logic other than their perception of the buyer's interaction with them.

In fact, many times relationship selling starts after the second sale.

Why? Because, when you talk about having a relationship with the prospect, you are not talking about how often they talk with you, meet with you, or respond to your e-mails. Relationship selling happens *after* the prospect has bought at least once from you, so they can determine if the value they received in the post-sales transaction is what you said would be delivered to them during the pre-sale discussions. It is during the post-sale that a buyer makes a judgment call and decides to have a business relationship with you by buying a second time.

So, when building out your sales forecasts, do not let salespeople build their forecast based on their

Chapter 10
Managing Forecasts

perception of the prospects' needs (their relationships). Often salespeople will "rainbow" their sales forecasts by projecting their needs onto the buyer rather than the actual action steps taken by the prospect towards an acquisition.

Accurate sales forecasts are crucial to company success. When you have an accurate sales forecast (over 80% accuracy), you can take it to the bank and get a line of credit. Sales forecasts drive your company's cash flow, staffing requirements, engineering needs, and marketing budget. When your sales forecast is incorrect, your entire department or company is affected.

As stated, a sales forecast is a snapshot of time that changes every day. To help manage the human emotion of sales forecasting by salespeople, you must use specific, quantifiable benchmarks to document transactional sales steps and measure sales forecasting accuracy.

Salespeople, by their very nature, are overly optimistic, so you need to manage their enthusiasm with a quantitative approach. For sales opportunities to be placed into a 90-day sales forecast, the account manager must be able to answer these questions correctly for you.

1. Does the prospect have a budget for your product or service? If so, how much?

2. Who is making the decision to buy?

Chapter 10
Managing Forecasts

3. Who is signing the purchase order or contract?

4. Who else will be involved in this decision (managers, steering committee, etc.)?

5. When does the prospect want to have this product or service (operational, installed, bought, and launched, in inventory, etc.)?

6. How will this purchase help the prospect's firm?

7. What will be the prospect's business consequences if they don't buy at all or if they buy from the wrong vendor? (This is called consequence management.)

If your salesperson cannot answer these questions correctly, <u>never</u> insert the sales opportunity into their sales forecast.

Some of your sales team will want to move their pipeline opportunities into their sales forecasts without answering all of these questions . . . but don't let them. By using this method, you will clean up the accuracy of your forecasts, while putting pressure on your sales team to move prospects from a sales pipeline opportunity into a qualified sales forecast opportunity.

When setting up your forecasts, you want to use a sales process that identifies action steps, thereby forcing your sales team members to quantify where they are in their sales metrics for each prospect opportunity.

1. Sales forecasts should be supplied by all salespeople at least monthly; but preferably weekly.

2. The sales forecast should be set up on 30-day, 60-day, and 90-day time lines. This is designed to identify sales closing barriers, a salesperson's progress, revenue projects, and business cash flow. By assigning a date (within 90 days) and a sales step approach, you are managing sales team members' inaccurate perceptions of where they think they are in the sales cycle.

3. All sales forecasts should be taken by management directly from a contact manager or Customer Relations Manager (CRM) system each Friday by 12:00 noon based on business deals with a 70% or higher probability of closing and <u>list the month they are anticipated to close.</u>

4. All information inserted in the contact manager/CRM after 12:00 noon each Friday will not be included in the Monday sales meeting forecast and will be posted to the following Friday's sales forecast.

NOTE: It is the responsibility of each employee (not the sales manager) who handles direct sales, partner sales, or renewal sales to insert updated prospect information and sales cycle probability in the contact manager/CRM on a daily basis.

Tightening the Sales Forecast

All accounts should be entered into the contact manager/CRM in the opportunity section, with the following probability percentages based on these sales steps and the projected close date.

100%   A signed agreement or purchase order has been received.

90%   Contract terms are being reviewed by the prospect's legal department or being negotiated.

80%   A verbal order where the paperwork will be done within 2 weeks, and the proposal and contracts have been submitted.

70%   The deal should be yours, but your competition is still present.

Differentiating Between a Forecast and a Pipeline

A **sales forecast** contains all prospects projected to be closed within 90 days that have an opportunity code of 70% or higher and meet the following qualifying questions:

1. The person you are working with is the decision maker and is signing the purchase order or contract.

2. The person you are working with has stated a budget and your product or service offering falls within the range of that stated budget.

3. The decision maker has told you that she will be buying a product or service like yours within 90 days.

A **sales pipeline** contains all prospects that have less than a 70% probability and will not be closed within 90 days. These should be inserted into the opportunity field with one of the following percentages and an estimated date to close.

60%	Active deal–competition is equal.
50%	Active deal this calendar year.
40%-10%	Prospective deals that may happen this calendar year.

Sales Forecast Example:

A product or service deal expected to be closed within 90 days, during the month of June, where you *should* win, but there is competition present, would be coded as "June 70%."

This approach of a metric-driven sales forecast based on sales steps tied to dates helps control the common problem many sales managers have called "sales projection." Sales projection is when sales team members "project" their needs—to sell, to increase their commissions, to hit their sales quotas, and in some cases, to keep their jobs—onto buyers. By packaging the sales forecast into quantitative sales steps, you minimize sales projection and increase the efficiency of your sales team.

You can use this basic format or develop your own based on the sales step requirements you have for an average product or service sale within your company.

The key to setting up a metric-based sales forecasting program is **tying the sales steps to time**.

Sales Closing Audit

The following form is an excellent sales management tool to help understand the knowledge your sales team members have about closing a specific prospect they have forecasted.

Chapter 10
Managing Forecasts

Sales Closing Audit

Today's date_____

Prospect/Client Name:_____

Contact Name:_____

Contact Title:_____

Person signing contract (if different from above):_____

Deal Value:_____

What are they buying?_____

Projected closing date:_____

What is their publicly stated budget?_____

Have you submitted your proposal yet? _____Yes _____No

Did you submit the proposal in person? _____Yes _____No

If no, how was proposal submitted? _____

Competitors in your deal_____
_____
_____

Last date of client contact:_____

Contact Method _____In-person _____Phone _____E-mail

Why will they buy?_____

Why will you lose?_____

Business consequence if they do not buy?_____

Next action step(s) _____By E-mail _____By phone _____In-person
_____
_____

Date of next action step_____

I need help from (circle all needed):

Operations   Sales Management   Senior Management   Service

Other _____

Chapter 11

Managing Sales by Metrics

After reading this chapter, you will know:

- Why metrics are so powerful in understanding your prospects and salesperson performance

- What metrics you can start measuring immediately

- How to evaluate your team's performance based on metrics rather than emotion

- How to monitor your team's strengths and weaknesses on a weekly, monthly, and quarterly basis

- How your team perceives their business value

Identifying Major Sales Metrics

If you have been involved in sales management for any period of time, you know that managing salespeople can be difficult. Some are whiners, some are professional politicians, some are lazy, and

Chapter 11
Managing Sales by Metrics

others rise to sales greatness far beyond your expectations and theirs.

One objective, non-emotional way to manage salespeople is to manage them by sales metrics. Metric management is a sales management tool that allows you to numerically measure salespeople to help align their action steps and your sales success expectations. Sales metrics also help you understand the skill sets of each of your sales team members and helps you develop sales training to fill any gaps in staff knowledge.

There are many sales metrics you can use to manage salespeople. Here are the major sales metrics that should be managed on a weekly or monthly basis for you to understand your sales team's effectiveness and training requirements. All of these can be measured on a weekly basis, but where appropriate, I have indicated when they can be measured monthly.

1. **Sales closing ratio by prospect title. (Monthly)**
   This metric measures your account managers' sales success in selling your product or service to specific titles (i.e., sales success to CFOs versus sales success to VPs of Operations).

2. **Average discount off submitted proposal price. (Monthly)**
   This metric tracks the average sales price range each salesperson sells at and their

ability to sell larger deals. It also measures their ability not to discount off current corporate pricing guidelines.

3. **Average discount off submitted proposal price by buyer's title. (Monthly)**
This metric tracks individual sales staff success in selling to VPs versus chief operating officers.

4. **Sales (in dollars) for each product and service sold per account sales manager. (Monthly)**
This metric tracks your sales team's focus on what specific product and service they like to sell and the success in dollars by offering type.

5. **Percent of closing ratio by product and service. (Weekly)**
This measures your account manager's sales success by product and service and number of separate deals sold per category.

6. **Percent of closing ratio by industry vertical. (Monthly)**
This metric tracks sales account managers' success by each industry they pursue to determine if there is a market focus imbalance (i.e., they prefer selling manufacturing instead of healthcare).

Chapter 11
Managing Sales by Metrics

7. **Average length of sales cycle (from lead to contract) in weeks for each product and service account managers sell. (Monthly)**
   This metric measures the average sales time for each account manager for each product and service they sell and helps sales management monitor sales forecasts for accuracies.

8. **Cold calls made per day to new prospects. (Weekly)**
   This metric measures how much a salesperson fills in the sales pipeline with opportunities from new prospects and also helps determine whether the salesperson is a Hunter or a Farmer.

9. **Cold calls made per day to existing customers. (Weekly)**
   This metric measures how much your salesperson fills in the sales pipeline with opportunities from existing customers and also helps determine whether the salesperson is a Hunter or a Farmer.

10. **The number of leads it takes to get one sale. (Monthly)**
    This metric tracks your ROI for marketing investment on a cost-per-lead basis.

Chapter 11
Managing Sales by Metrics

11. **Overall closing ratios for all proposals submitted. (Monthly)**
This metric measures your sales staff's overall success as a percent of proposals submitted.

12. **Size of sales forecasts for each account manager based on individual closing ratios. (Monthly)**
This measurement tracks the potential for your sales staff to hit their sales forecast based on individual closing ratios. For example, if a sales rep's quota is $1,000,000 per year and she has a 25% closing ratio for proposals submitted, then she needs $4,000,000 in proposals in her sales forecast to hit her quota.

13. **Separate all sales staff into two separate categories (1) those with more than 3 years of experience in your firm and (2) those with less than 3 years experience. Evaluate each against the peers in the same category.**
This measurement will help you individually evaluate and compare salespeople with their peers. Comparing a ten-year sales veteran in your firm against a two-year sales veteran in your firm is not a balanced approach.

Chapter 11
Managing Sales by Metrics

14. **Number of first appointments made per month with qualified prospects. (Monthly)**
    This metric measures your sales team's month-to-month effectiveness on getting new appointments.

15. **Number of second meetings, executive briefings, or demos completed per month with qualified prospects. (Monthly)**
    This metric measures your sales team's month-to-month effectiveness on moving prospects forward to the next sales step.

16. **Lost sales by type of sales objection.** This metric measures the impact specific sales objections have on closing deals.

17. **Discount percentage by title sold.** This metric measures the negotiating skill your team has with specific business titles.

18. **Discount percentage by business industry sold.** This metric measures industry profitability for your product or service.

19. **Overall closing ratio by deal dollar size.** This metric measures the salesperson's negotiating skills based on the value of the deal.

20. **Leads generated by networking**. This metric quantifies networking value.

21. **Leads generated by marketing**. This metric measures the return on marketing investments.

A sales strategy without an execution plan is like a boat without a paddle . . . you can see the horizon, but you just can't get there from where you are at.

Evaluating Your Sales Team's Performance

Evaluating your sales team's successes and failures from a metric point of view is as important as the theoretical perception of what you need to do to hit your firm's sales forecasts based on the understanding of your market.

Anyone who has ever managed a sales team knows that sales quota success is not just tied to the team's sales skills, but is also influenced by how your firm markets and positions its products and services.

**Having a sales strategy is good,
but having a sales execution plan is better!**

Understanding the business metrics of your firm's sales team is one of the keys to increasing sales.

In many ways, managing a sales team is a mathematical model.

Chapter 11
Managing Sales by Metrics

In the day-to-day pressure of managing a sales team, VPs of Sales do not have the luxury of gathering or studying their sales team's metrics. Most sales executives can quote their teams' average closing ratio or standard deal value, but other data is absent. Due to the pressure of trying to help their teams hit quota, most VPs of Sales or sales managers <u>are too busy</u> to analyze their teams' mathematical sales models. Yet, if they did, their teams would be more successful.

To be able to sell more, your firm's marketing or administrative department should help the vice president of sales calculate sales team business metrics on a quarterly basis. With this data, you can slice and dice your sales team's analysis and make appropriate adjustments in training, employment, product and service pricing, and market growth opportunities. You can also use this data to make rational and fair business decisions on individual team member's ability to sell under changing sales metrics.

Henry Clay once said, "Statistics are no substitute for judgment."

Remember, by using both good sales statistics and good judgment, you can sell more and know why.

Remember, the salesperson's paradigm: The buying cycle and selling cycle are never the same.

Chapter 11
Managing Sales by Metrics

Here are five reasons most firms miss their revenue goals:

1. Sales quota is inaccurate
2. Firm is product, service or feature-driven
3. Sales model is wrong
4. Firm uses relationship marketing, not transactional marketing
5. Market demand was not calculated

Sales Team Monthly Assessment

Use the following assessment guideline to monitor your sales team member skills to help you identify their strengths, weaknesses, and areas needing training.

Chapter 11
Managing Sales by Metrics

Sales Team Monthly Skill Assessment

Account Manager's Name_____ Month_____

Cold Calling
Cold calls to new prospects .... _____
Cold calls to existing customers... _____
Converting cold calls to appointments .... _____

Demos
Number of presentations per month .... _____
Number of webinars per month.. _____
Presentation conversion to proposals .... _____

Qualifying Prospects
Appointments with contract signer .... _____
Prospects have stated a budget .... _____
Prospects have stated an operational date......................... _____
Prospects have stated a business pain or problem .... _____
Prospects have communicated your competition .... _____

Decision Influencer Management
Know why they will buy from you .... _____
Know why you will lose business .... _____
Identified who is influencing the contract signer .... _____
Know the political issues of the sale .... _____
Establish rapport with decision influencer........................... _____
Understand how the decision is being made (RFP, etc.) .... _____
Has decision influencer verbalized your business value..... _____

Decision Maker/Contract Signer Management
Know why they will buy from you .... _____
Know why you will lose the business .... _____
Establish rapport with contract signer .... _____
Has decision maker verbalized your business value .... _____

Proposals
Proposals always approved by operations and/or accurate .... _____

Negotiation
Needs minimal help with deal negotiations......................... _____
Closing ratio from proposal is 28% or better....................... _____
Negotiation discount is within company guidelines............. _____

Sales Forecasting
Month-to-month sales forecast is at least 75% accurate .... _____
Sales forecasts are submitted timely .... _____

CRM/Contact Manager Maintenance
Enters data into CRM daily .... _____
CRM data is accurate and detailed...................................... _____

Expense Management
Expenses are submitted on time.. _____
Receipts are submitted with expense reports .... _____

Team Support
Works with team member positively .... _____

Chapter 11
Managing Sales by Metrics

Take the following Revenue Capture Value Test to see how your team sees their business value. Give this test to your sales team and sell they score.

Revenue Capture Value Test

1. Do you sell your firm's product and service horizontally to everyone, or do you sell vertically to specific markets?

    ____Horizontally ____Vertically

2. Do your get asked to drop your price more than 50% of the time by prospects before they will buy?

    ____Yes ____No

3. When you lose a deal, do prospects tell you more than 50% of the time that your price was too high?

    ____Yes ____No

4. Do you lead with price as your sales value proposition when presenting to a prospect?

    ____Yes ____No

5. Do you have a standard price discount you are allowed to give to a prospect without management approval in order to close a deal?

    ____Yes ____No

6. Do you get paid on gross margin or gross revenue?

    ____Gross Margin ____Gross Revenue

7. Is the word *price* mentioned anywhere on your website, advertising, sales brochures, or standard sales letters to prospects?

    ____Yes ____No

Chapter 11
Managing Sales by Metrics

8. After seeing your proposal and all of your competitors, in the final sales cycle steps prior to closing your deals, do prospects ask you to explain why you are different more than 50% of the time?

    ____Yes ____No

9. Are your pricing metrics based on your competitors' prices?

    ____Yes ____No

10. On repeat sales to existing clients, do your clients hold you hostage for discounts to get add-on business?

    ____Yes ____No

Correct Answers:

1) Vertically   2) No   3) No   4) No   5) No

6) Gross Margin   7) No   8) No   9) No   10) No

Scoring:

Each correct answer gets 10 points. Each incorrect answer gets 0 points. Now add up your score.

Chapter 12

Managing Strategic Alliances and Channel Partners

After reading this chapter, you will know:

- Why alliance and partner sales are long-term revenue enhancers

- What collectives are and how you can benefit from them

- How to develop and manage strategic alliances and channel partners for productive relationships

Understanding Strategic Replication— Alliance Partner Collectives

Developing strategic partnerships and alliances to help increase your company's product and service sales is a key business process for many industries and an important goal for sales management.

It is important to remember two sales management variables concerning revenue capture:

1. Direct sales are short- and long-term revenue enhancers for companies.

2. Partner and channel sales are long-term revenue enhancers.

It takes time and money to generate prospect sales from strategic channel partners. Partners' sales success will be directly dependent on your firm's sales team success and delivery of your sales and marketing programs.

Partners and channel alliances are common, but studies of alliances in different industries reveal that many of these "strategic" alliances are not strategic at all. In fact, many of the alliances become wasted energy and a true loss of revenue opportunity that may have been successful if a more traditional business model had been used to evaluate and deploy alliances.

Today, business alliances need to be managed with a more logical model approach. Deploying strategic alliance relationships correctly can help small firms appear big and generate true identifiable revenue streams that can be managed and enlarged. Conversely, correct strategic alliances for larger firms can help fill market gaps that smaller firms may be filling.

Much like the affiliate market for e-commerce sales, such as books and information, business alliances can offer companies the ability to sell their services and products at lower sales capture cost while spreading the distribution and advertising expenses over other firms' G&A overhead.

By introducing strategic alliance concepts to the old channel-partner responsibilities, you add additional expansion capabilities.

Successful strategic alliances are more like a business utopian format that increases the value of the individual players by being a part of **a larger collective**. (A "collective" is the integration with your partner's partners.)

When strategic alliances work, they become a self-replicating revenue machine as one partnership leads to another and each new partner adds value and sales leads to the team.

In today's economy, a true strategic alliance executive needs to have a hybrid of skill sets, including experiences that cover major account sales, marketing, strategy, contract negotiations, and deal making.

A <u>strategic alliance collective</u> allows each firm to contribute to the business roll-up by having its firm enhanced by the association with the partners and allows new partners to benefit simultaneously, stimulating a continuous introduction of other partners outside of the originating collective.

Strategic Alliance Collective Partnership Example:

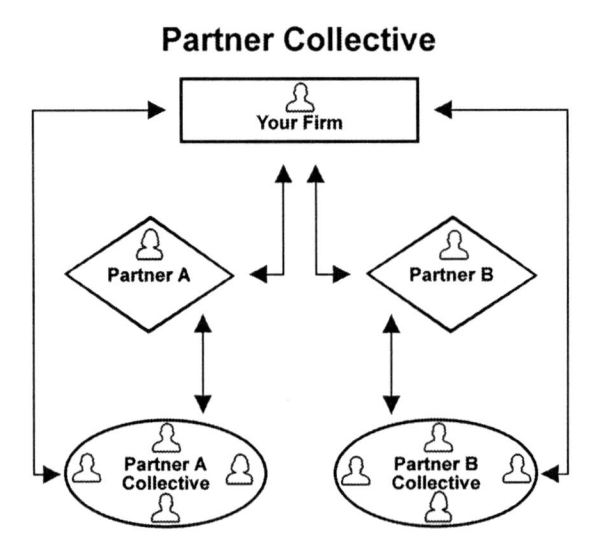

Partner Collective

[Diagram: Your Firm at top, connected to Partner A and Partner B, each connected to their respective Partner Collectives]

Thus, smart product and service collectives are always self-replicating as they grow by association and alliance success. In successful partnerships, they are as loyal to you as you are to them. Help them make money and they will bring you more business and sales leads; ignore them and you will get no attention.

Chapter 12
Managing Strategic Alliances and Channel Partners

Strategic Partner Management—Rules to Guide Alliances and Collectives to Increase Sales

1. **Do not over-negotiate.** Most firms that launch strategic alliances usually do not make sure the deal is mutually beneficial. Everyone is so excited about getting "the deal," they don't try to equally maximize the gain for the partner they just aligned with. If you over-negotiate, the partner may ultimately feel that the relationship is unbalanced and will not introduce you to more collective partners (or sales leads).

2. **Find out how big the potential alliance partner's collective is before you cut the deal.** See beyond the immediate partnership. Who does your potential alliance partner with? The endgame may not be the immediate partner, but the doors they can open for you. Like dominos, strategic alliances are all interconnected. Think of the collective as a self-replicating model, not a self-maximizing model. Let your partners introduce you to their partners.

3. **Strategic alliances are about revenue only.** Let's learn from the mistakes of others—it is substance over PR that counts in partnerships. If a strategic alliance

cannot ultimately create revenue, either directly or through collective introductions or sales leads, then you are wasting your time. Set up financial and lead generation metric goals that are used as a scorecard to measure your alliance's success.

4. **Roll up, not down.** Create new markets, generate new customers, fill existing product and service gaps, but always build up your business. The right alliance collective is like building a new holding company. The goal is to roll up many businesses and create a larger competitive mass. If you are cutting small deals, you will always be a little company.

5. **You must have commitment by the strategic partner's senior management.** No matter how small your firm is or how big your alliance partner is, if your management team can't meet an executive or vice president to discuss the details, then your alliance will never maximize its revenue opportunities. Senior management of large companies will always meet you <u>if your deal is important to them</u>.

6. **You must have senior management commitment in your firm.** Your firm needs commitment in people, time, and money for this to work. In order to receive commitment from partners, you have to be

committed as well. If establishing relationships is regarded as busy work, it will ultimately fail. Remember, strategic partner sales are long-term revenue opportunities.

7. **This is marriage, not serial dating.** Take time to foster and expand. Companies won't invite you inside their partner collective if you are involved with them one day and gone the next.

8. **Although this is marriage, it may not be monogamous.** The key to good strategic alliances is to keep <u>enlarging your collective alliance model</u>. With these continually increasing concentric circles of influence, at times there will be an overlap of your relationships. You may have to make choices, trading up from one collective partnership circle to a larger opportunity. This trade-up can be effective, but also destructive. If you attempt this, you need to evaluate the option carefully based on the human, operational, and capital investments you have already spent on the introducing collective or collective partner.

9. **Timing is important.** You have learned that being first to market does not always work. Often being first means higher development costs, greater sales capture

costs, and a smaller target market of early buyers. To be first with a large partner can leapfrog your firm deep into their realm of collective influences and maximize your ROI quickly. In alliance development, timing is important as well, but by leaping first, you can also expose your firm to the partner's lack of preparation and ability to respond. Move quickly, but **make sure the partner is ready**.

10. **Mutual financial commitments are a must.** There are few successful strategic partnerships where one or both firms do not ultimately exchange money for services rendered. It can be payment for training, sharing trade show costs, minimum product or service purchases, or co-op direct mail. Somewhere there has to be funding exchanges to seal the deal. PR alliances don't work. Business costs money. If there are no mutual-flowing purchase requirements, then you are really not striking a true alliance deal. Sharing leads without a financial commitment is usually pretty weak.

11. **When selecting strategic partners, less is more.** Many firms feel that the more alliances they create, the better off they are. You should think like a sharpshooter and strategically pick direct collective

Chapter 12
Managing Strategic Alliances and Channel Partners

players that fit well with your goals. Maintaining a strong alliance requires a full-time person dedicated to each relationship with 100 percent backing of their firm's infrastructure. That is a lot of bandwidth for any company.

Strategic partnerships are the building blocks to long-term growth. Just make sure that the growth is a planned process.

Chapter 12
Managing Strategic Alliances and Channel Partners

Chapter 13

Using Sales Scorecards to Manage More Effectively

After reading this chapter, you will know:

- Why scorecards can help you meet your corporate goals

- How to prepare and implement a sales scorecard

The world is entering into a paradigm shift for business creation and ongoing growth—the opportunity for companies to continue growing is becoming dependent on their ability to generate internal profits to fund expansion.

When you have an increasing demand for internal corporate cash, paired with an increasing demand for capital investments to grow your top-line revenue, you create a vortex where funding has exceeded business requirements. This vortex is forcing many companies to miss business milestones, established players to reduce fixed costs, and mature firms to sell assets. As companies miss their management teams, investor milestones, or Wall Street commitments, they reduce their business valuation and subordinate their ability to succeed and fund growth. The crucial issue for growth-directed companies in today's economy is to meet predetermined revenue milestones on time and on budget.

In a world where increased revenue has become an executive mantra, turning business plan strategy into actionable steps that create revenue has become, for some, an albatross.

The key to success is to continually increase internal funding capabilities and help reduce dependence on third-party funding resources. For companies to continually grow, business units must quickly produce tangible sales results. One methodology to accomplish this is through a **Sales Scorecard.**

Like other scorecard concepts, the success of the Sales Scorecard is driving fundamental business changes. By creating identifiable tactical measures for each of your sales team members and contributing departments, you can transform silo performance into group performance and create a pattern for integrated sales team performance.

Sales Scorecards are sub-segments of the original scorecard concept currently used by approximately 60% of Fortune 1000 companies. The original premise of the scorecard is based on linking, intersecting, and managing four distinct business perspectives. The scorecard process is presently used as a centralized business implementation and strategy tool. The success behind the scorecard methodology is based on its ability to transcend executive philosophies and help departments become more productive as a team from the boardroom to the mailroom.

Unlike other management philosophies, the sales scorecard is not a static business concept. Instead, it is a continuously changing management tool that allows companies to adapt to market conditions as they develop. Unlike **M**anagement **B**y **O**bjective (MBO) theorems where corporations are focused on changing behavior by <u>studying yesterday's performance</u> to bring about modification for today, the scorecard model focuses on today and tomorrow and those elements that can turn <u>present strategy into future action</u>. Through the utilization of the Sales Scorecard, businesses can manage sales team's performance based on today's information and react to tomorrow's market changes and sales success needs.

The scorecard is not just a static list of metrics or isolated Key Performance Indicators (KPIs). Instead, it is a graphical framework for implementing and aligning sales tactics and managing strategy for companies seeking to become successful.

Businesses must manage their capital capabilities to succeed.

Chapter 13
Using Sales Scorecards to Manage More Effectively

Today, most companies can break down their corporate assets into three specific areas, which include:

1. Human capital (employees)

2. Operational capital (product and service development and delivery)

3. Financial capital (business funding, revenue, monthly burn rate, valuation, corporate revenue, A/R, line of credit)

With these capital elements always at risk for companies, it becomes crucial for management to develop a strategic blueprint for all employees to work together. The Sales Scorecard is such a program, but it integrates five areas rather than four. Through its implementation, line and staff associates interact weekly as a packaged team to help drive performance and create revenue as a group instead of traditional department silos.

Five sales management pillars to track are:

1. Sales

2. Marketing

3. Strategy

4. Product Development/Operations

5. Strategic Partners/Alliances

Chapter 13
Using Sales Scorecards to Manage More Effectively

Understanding the Sales Scorecard Concept

The Sales Scorecard is the intersection of the five business elements that contribute to revenue. Through these intersections of department responsibilities, the <u>entire team becomes accountable to create revenue</u> and is motivated by a common corporate goal.

Let's again review the following questions:

- Why should sales be held accountable if the marketing department cannot generate qualified leads?

- Why should the sales department be held responsible because the strategy department incorrectly forecast a market gap size?

- Why should the sales department be held accountable if the strategic partner or channel manager generates no leads from existing alliances?

- Why should the sales department be measured on revenue for selling blue cars, when customers want red cars?

It is important to understand that revenue generation in companies is a cause-and-effect process. Revenue will be short without a market-driven product, services to sell, or appropriate positioning support.

Chapter 13
Using Sales Scorecards to Manage More Effectively

Success will be minimized if the focus is placed on the sales department as the primary driver for revenue shortfall rather than identifying and fixing the primary problem. The Sales Scorecard is a visual measurement device used to view the integrated variables of revenue generation from all salespeople. Additionally, by identifying all sales tactics needed to sell and/or non-contributions as they happen, you can make adjustments to your sales team's current behavior before it is too late and identify help from other departments that may be needed.

Why these five indicators?

The Sales Scorecard—like other scorecards—it takes strategic objectives and translates them into specific key performance indicators (KPIs). Each element of the sales development five-pillar program can directly increase or decrease corporate sales revenue. Most firms isolate and focus on only one department (like sales) for revenue responsibility, which only hides the shared responsibility of supporting departments.

The five elements all contribute directly to the success or failure of revenue generation. By monitoring each of these elements individually and intertwined with the scorecard's goal of increased revenue, you can adapt to sales issues before they become barriers.

How is the Sales Scorecard set up?

The Sales Scorecard starts with an <u>accurate corporate sales budget</u>. From here, all strategy flows into tactical executions using the business plan details as monthly benchmarks tied to capital capability deployment. What makes a Sales Scorecard easier to develop than most scorecard deployments is that the focus is highly defined. It supplies a graphical picture of where you are and where you need to be.

Remember, <u>revenue is revenue.</u>

The Sales Scorecard is more than a sales project plan. It is a working battle plan to create interdepartmental collaboration to achieve tactical revenue goals simultaneously. It links interdepartmental success to corporate success and corporate revenue. It makes a sales forecast the company's responsibility rather than the sales department's.

Using a **Sales Scorecard**, you <u>link</u> multiple departments' responsibilities to the creation of revenue. Using this approach, the firm's business assets are centralized on revenue development and all departments are linked to that performance. With this linkage, the Sales Scorecard provides clarity in its strategic and tactical goals.

Preparing a Sales Scorecard

Using the sales plan as the starting source of data, the format for the Sales Scorecard is as follows:

1. Separate the sales revenue commitment listed on the annual sales forecast into monthly goals (as you already do). Almost all of the plan's tactical elements will be cross-represented into department perspectives and responsibilities. Then, assign specific metrics on a monthly basis to each of the five department heads as criteria of their success.

   How is a Sales Scorecard different from a sales or monthly objective plan?

   It is different because you link <u>company revenue as a team objective</u>, setting measurement (and compensation) to the goal accomplished <u>as a group</u>. By having all departments linked together in pursuit of the same corporate goal—increased monthly revenue—decisions become more focused.

   Monthly Metric—Five Areas to Be Measured

   a) Sales Perspectives

   b) Marketing Perspectives

Chapter 13
Using Sales Scorecards to Manage More Effectively

    c) Strategy Perspectives

    d) Product Development/Operations Perspectives

    e) Alliances/Partnerships Perspectives

2. Once you have broken the plan commitments into one of the five perspectives, then subdivide each process, attaching the departmental responsibility for its completion and align the responsibility for <u>monthly</u> metrics to the department head.

Example:

Monthly corporate revenue plan goal—$2,000,000

A. Sales Perspectives

- Book $1,000,000 in new client business
- Book $500,000 in existing client business
- Meet with the top 3 clients
- Go on 5 sales calls with the sales staff
- Maintain 40% gross margin

B. Marketing Perspectives

- Obtain 100 qualified sales leads
- Hold an executive seminar for new prospects

Chapter 13
Using Sales Scorecards to Manage More Effectively

C. Strategy Perspectives

- Publish new competitive reports
- Publish a white paper on the new product

D. Product Development/Operations Perspectives

- Develop new feature list for enhancement insertion
- Hire new engineering staff

E. Alliances/Partnerships Perspectives

- Generate $500,000 from alliance sales
- Attend trade shows with alliance partners
- Generate 50 leads from alliance members

3. After each department's responsibilities have identified, then focus on the specific tasks and time allocation needed to reach the objective goal.

Example:

A. Sales Perspectives

- Cold call 50 customers per week
- Make presentations to 10 customers per week
- Close 2 sales per week

B. Marketing Perspectives

- Hold an executive seminar on third week of the month

C. Strategy Perspectives

- Interview 3 customers this week

D. Product Development/Operations Perspective

- Complete new product functionality review by the 1st of the month

E. Alliances/Partnerships Perspectives

- Review 2 new partner contracts with your legal department by the 15th of the month

4. Assign each task to a specific associate or manager who will be responsible, accountable, and measured weekly.

5. Lay out a detailed weekly milestone chart, in a spreadsheet such as Excel, to list individual assignments by departments, completion goalposts, and associates assigned the responsibility.

6. Last, add the three business assets of financial, operational, and human capital on top of each business plan goalpost to determine where an asset fulfillment capability gap exists.

On your Excel spreadsheet, **color-code** the assigned tasks as follows: "completed" in **green**, "uncompleted" in **red**, and "in progress" in **yellow**. At this junction, the Sales Scorecard becomes the pivotal information tool for all managers who individually and collectively can now see how the organization progresses week by week and how their performances are linked together as a team.

Now, complete a Sales Scorecard for each one of the business objectives listed in your plan.

Implementing the Sales Scorecard

On Fridays, have all department managers submit a task status to an office administrator for input in the scorecard. On Monday, hold a managers meeting and discuss the scorecard measurements with all managers interacting together to collectively achieve the business plan milestones.

As a sales manager, focus first on color coded yellow and red categories annotated in the Sales Scorecard. This category highlights the inability for department managers and salespeople to complete their job tasks based on available assets. Once the yellow designation areas are reviewed, move on to the red and then the green sections to determine the next steps.

Chapter 13
Using Sales Scorecards to Manage More Effectively

Having associates understand their weekly goals and interacting as a team, based on published expectations, will increase corporate moral and business resolution. The key for any company to succeed and meet the milestones of their investors or management team is for all departments to work together as a team to create revenue. In a market where many employees work fifty or more hours a week, the Sales Scorecard can be the vortex where strategy turns into action. By linking department performance together as a group, you will increase milestone execution and simultaneously increase corporate revenue.

The Sales Scorecard is a graphical business tool to help sales management integrate company departments into one outbound revenue capture program.

Chapter 13
Using Sales Scorecards to Manage More Effectively

Sales Scorecard Example:

Sales Scorecard				
Date	1-Jul	8-Jul	15-Jul	22-Jul
Timetable	Week 1	Week 2	Week 3	Week 4
Sales Dept. / George				
Cold Calls				
Presentations				
Closed Deals				
Hire New Reps				

Operations Dept. / Steve				
Install Customer Sites				
Held Training				
Wrote documentation update				

Accounting Dept. / Julie				
Paid Expenses on time				
Collected A/R under 30				
Reviewed all proposals within 3 days				
Released budgets for hiring				

Development Dept. / Frank				
Completed new release				
Completed customer demos				
Hired new reps				

Administrative Dept. / Anne				
Collected Scorecard info on time				
Created weekly Scorecards on time				

Marketing Dept. / Carolyn				
Sent direct mail				
Completed draft of brochure copy				
Sent out press release				

Chapter 14

Integrated Pillar Management

After reading this chapter, you will know:

- Why integrating sales, marketing, strategy, operations and strategy alliances improves your company's revenue performance

- How to integrate the five pillars for an effective revenue program

- What to expect from other department heads as they adjust to a new organizational structure

Integrating the Pillars

Integrated Pillar Management is a sales management approach designed to create a revenue capture program for all management.

The development and deployment of this program in its entirety is directly dependent on the title of the person reading this book and the influence you have in your firm and with your senior management team.

There are two approaches to this program deployment. The first approach is through a best practice review and ROI basis, working with each department head to build consensus and revenue maximization. I'll refer to this approach as the ROI Approach. The second (and more preferred method) is to adjust your entire revenue program from a top-down approach to integrate the pillar departments as an integrated program. I'll refer to this approach as the Top-Down Approach.

To be honest, it is never easy for a company to deploy a corporate-wide sales management program because of the existing inertia of the old methods—**but this is the future**.

The entire company—not just the vice president of sales—is responsible for sales.

In many ways, **old is good**. We have been taught this from the dot-com "experts" who spent a disproportionate amount of their VC funding on dumb ads for major sporting events and called it "branding." Branding without revenue is just wasted money.

We have learned from companies which had great catchy names, but no revenue models, that company names without revenue does not make any sense.

Additionally, we also have learned that signing business partnerships to generate press releases instead of ultimately generating leads for your sales team is not productive.

The art of generating corporate revenue is always challenging and needs to be adapted to the continuing business environment in which you operate.

By deploying the Integrated Pillar Management, you are seeking to introduce a new model for revenue integration.

I am going to focus on the second approach for two reasons. First, the ROI Approach is a sub-segment of the Top-Down Approach and is implemented on a department-by-department basis by focusing on the ROI discussion and tools previously reviewed for each of the five pillars. With the ROI Approach, you set each staff position as a line position and slowly move them to an integrated model. Second, the Top-Down Approach is more complex to implement.

In order to integrate the Top-Down Approach to a successful sales management program, you need to follow these guidelines:

1. **Executive Sponsorship. The CEO/President or senior executive in charge must be involved.** Not having senior management sponsorship will only create dissention among the management types involved and will cause the senior

executive implementing this program to fail.

Can Senior VPs of Sales and Marketing implement this program by themselves? **Yes.** If the vice president of sales has direct staff that is responsible for marketing, strategy, and strategic alliances, as well as sales, this can be implemented.

Once you decide to implement this program, you must **commit wholeheartedly.** You cannot be weak in the knees. <u>You must be a Hunter.</u>[3] This is a totally different revenue model currently in use–so you must believe.

Like other executive initiatives, assign yourself an appropriate time formula to implement. If you are in the middle of a fiscal year, you may want to implement the basic model in stages, in anticipation of complete integration when the fiscal year budgeting is being planned.

Be aware that this program is going to change how you forecast business, generate revenue, and pay people. This will be a **BIG cultural** change for all involved–so go slowly.

---

[3] See my book, *Value Forward Selling: How to Sell to Management* located at www.howtoselltomanagement.com.

2. **Revenue Responsibilities.** In a traditional Global 1000 organizational environment, positions like strategy and marketing are staff positions that support line positions like sales. Many times these supporting positions report directly to the senior executive. **This is a mistake**. The vice president of sales is held accountable for revenue that at times is controlled by support staff, who may make counter-revenue decisions based on how they are evaluated and paid. So, the first step is to turn all pillar executive management positions into **LINE POSITIONS.** This way, they are now accountable and allocated the same business respect for that accountability.

    Do they still report to the senior sales executive? That is open for debate based on your company's current organizational and political structure, but they all need to report to the same person so there is group responsibility for revenue.

3. **Quotas.** All sales, marketing, strategy, operations, and strategic alliance managers should now have dollar quotas. **These individual quotas will link all of them together into a collective decision process to generate revenue**. All decisions by the departments will be tied to

one question: "Will my actions generate short- or long-term revenue for the company?" Under this model, the vice president of sales can still hit or miss his quota, but now he will have supporting management executives reinforcing him in his effort.

4. **Quota Determination.** Generating quotas for all of the business development pillar managers must be determined and based on real world calculations, not backroom magic. Since marketing, strategy, and alliances managers are not generally used to having 50% of their income derived from a quota-based system, they need confidence in the potential attainment of the quota and comfort that their numbers are logical.

5. **Quota Assignment.** What should the revenue quota for the vice president of marketing and the manager of alliances be? The pivotal questions are: "Should their quotas be included in the company's total sales quota normally assigned to the vice president of sales?" or "Should their quotas be **ADDED to the vice president of sales' quota for a new, higher group quota?**" Each method has value, but in a new business development launch program, it is better to have their quotas serve as

Chapter 14
Integrated Pillar Management

contributing parts of the entire vice president of sales' quota. Once your outbound sales management pillar program has completed one fiscal year, then you should have each pillar manager's quota calculated as a separate total. This way, during your program launch year, your vice president of sales can still hit her quota, even if the other contributing managers fail.

(a) First twelve months of the sales management pillar program: the senior managers of marketing, strategy, and strategic alliances assigned quotas are sub-segments of the vice president of sales' quota.

(b) Second twelve months of the sales management pillar program: each five-pillar manager has her own individual quota.

6. **Compensation.** Like sales executives, marketing, strategy, operations, and alliance executives should be paid a base salary and commissions based on the revenue they personally (or their departments) generate as a percentage of quota. Their base salary (like most VPs of Sales) should only be 50% of their total compensation. Under the quota system of compensation, the executives in charge of

marketing, strategy, operations, and strategic alliances need to make more. Should their comp plan increase? Yes. Should their comp plan increases be tied to revenue? Yes.

7. **Business Controls.** Most VPs of Sales have profit margin and proposal approval guidelines. Similarly, all members of the pillars of sales management must have business controls inserted in their comp plans so their business decisions are ***not only*** driven by revenue, ***but also*** driven by good business logic. You are not seeking revenue for the sake of revenue, but smart and profitable revenue.

8. **Documentation.** All quotas, compensation plans, and common control mechanisms for the pillar sales management executives must be in writing.

9. **Assignment of Tasks.** As compensation plans change, it is imperative that you develop specific task assignments for each pillar department manager (marketing, product development) to measure their goal successes. As reviewed previously, you need to measure each department's tasks in finite and ROI capability. This way, you eliminate vagueness and focus on directed actions they should take to generate revenue.

Chapter 14
Integrated Pillar Management

10. **Job Descriptions.** The future of modern sales management is the acceptance of this group quota concept. To turn traditional staff positions like marketing and strategy into line positions, you must assign them responsibilities based on their understanding of the new jobs as outlined specifically in their job descriptions. To do this, you must work with your HR department to develop job descriptions that focus on revenue generation and responsibility assignment, much like a vice president of sales job description. I've provided an example job description for a vice president of marketing on the following page.

Chapter 14
Integrated Pillar Management

Example Job Description Based on Integrated Pillar Management:

VP of Marketing

Reports To: CEO/President
Direct Reports: All marketing staff
Quota Assignment: Annual quota is $8 million
Compensation
   Base Salary: $110,000 paid bi-weekly
   Commissions: 1% of gross revenue paid monthly on ROI calculations of marketing programs

Position Description:

The VP of Marketing is directly responsible for 100% or greater attainment of their assigned annual revenue quota as currently determined by the executive committee. The VP of Marketing will manage, train, support, and direct all marketing staff as needed to reach their department's revenue quota. Additionally, the VP of Marketing will maintain a positive work environment with all work associates and will interact with all managers at all levels as needed.

Functional Job Requirements:

The VP of Marketing's functional responsibilities will include, but are not limited to:

- Interacting with the pillars of the business development team for company quota attainment issues.
- Holding weekly revenue forecasting and ROI meetings with all marketing staff to confirm quota year-to-date status.
- Submitting appropriate revenue forecasting as needed to the executive committee.
- Calculate marketing ROI for all project programs prior to launch.
- Interacting with the executive committee on a weekly basis or as directed.
- Supporting and maintaining all company human resources policies as directed by the HR employee manual.
- Reviewing all marketing staff expense report traffic within the company stated T&E guideline and the department's forecasted expense budgets.
- Interacting with all existing major accounts as needed to extend recurring revenue relationships.
- Reviewing each assigned employee's performance on a semi-annual basis as outlined in the HR manual.

Chapter 14
Integrated Pillar Management

As you can see by this new job description for the vice president of marketing, the position has been elevated to a **LINE position** directly attached to a revenue quota.

You now have a management group whose job functions and compensation plan centers around revenue generation as a team.

The group needs to meet once a week, separately from other executive meetings, to collectively make decisions on revenue-generation opportunities. They need to submit their assigned completed tasks and goals to an administrator to be inserted into their **Sales Scorecard** for measurement and discussion. (See Chapter 13 for Sales Scorecard development.)

At least one day each week, the managers should meet to discuss business opportunities and how they can maximize revenue as a team (all motivated by a common goal–their centralized quota and compensation plans).

That's it.

Sounds easy, right? Not really. Due to your firm's pressure to continue to live under the traditional Fortune 500 organizational structure, that keeps line and staff positions separated, you will find tremendous pressure not to change. Staff managers who are being held accountable for revenue for the first time will not like this structure or compensation model.

Chapter 14
Integrated Pillar Management

Calculating ROI, quota, and tactical tasks for strategy, and operations, strategic alliances, and marketing managers will be an involved, interactive, and cumbersome process. I recommend you use your CFO or vice president of finance with each of the managers as a mediator, to collectively have them determine what a fair quota is. Getting a "green light" from the management team is required for the five-pillar system to work.

But—here is the key business driver—if your firm does not adapt its business model to an integrated, outbound sales management program, you will never reach your full revenue potential. Instead, your existing Fortune 500 organizational structure of rigid demarcation between line and staff positions will reinforce dysfunctional business decisions and continue to waste funding on non-ROI validated expenses.

Something to think about!

Should it be a goal? Yes definitely, but a mid- to long-term goal (up to one year), where the vice president of operations is paid commission on gross revenues. Although this would be a culture shock to the group, it would be better to postpone this potential integration and wait for your success with the initial four managers of the business development pillar team (sales, marketing, strategy and alliances).

Chapter 14
Integrated Pillar Management

6-Week Implementation Plan

The following plan is designed to help your firm develop and deploy an integrated pillar management program from a top-down approach, company-wide to help sales management increase their success. Using the outline for a 6-week program, you can follow the recommendations and slowly build your business case and methodology to bring about corporate consensus between both the managers involved as well as the associated department heads.

NOTE: The vice president of sales is involved in all meetings of the five-pillar business development group, even when not noted.

Week One

- Meet with the executives in charge of strategy, operations, sales, marketing, and alliances to discuss the pillar management concept. The executive team should be present to handle general conversations and to communicate why your firm needs to evolve toward this goal.

- Review your sales forecasting methods and determine your firm's true sales opportunities based on cumulative territory potentials.

- Ask the executives from strategy, operations, marketing, and alliances to develop a list of ten variables they think can be measured from a ROI and revenue generation point of view.

- Have the CFO and/or vice president of finance set up appointments with these staff managers to help them calculate the variables.

- Ask the HR department to draft new job descriptions for each manager.

Week Two

- Hold a second group meeting with the executive team and the business development group to discuss last week's conversation and ongoing investigations.

- Have the strategy, operations, marketing, and alliances managers submit the ten elements for ROI calculations they think can be measured and attached to a budgeted quota to the executive committee.

- Have the CFO review the ROI numbers and determine a measuring system to calculate and document these numbers.

- Review the new job description drafts from HR in the executive committee.

Week Three

- Have all executives who are involved reconfirm that the sales forecast calculations

Chapter 14
Integrated Pillar Management

are reasonable based on market potential approach.

- Determine the quota assignments for the strategy, operations, marketing, and alliance managers. If you have done your due diligence looking at ROI by department, these numbers will be reasonably accepted by the department heads.

- Once the quota assignments are determined, insert them into the managers' new job description drafts supplied by HR.

- Review the new job description drafts with the managers.

- Review with the CFO how the ROIs will be tracked and what paperwork the department heads need to submit in order to help with the calculations.

- Review the new compensation plans for the managers. New base salaries and commission payouts should be postponed for 90 days, while the program is launched, to help confirm the measurement methodologies and to work out any snags.

- If there is going to be a new organizational structure reflecting the changes of staff executives to line executives, have the CEO send an e-mail to everyone in the company announcing the organizational changes and the associated business logic.

- Insert the metrics developed from your new quota assignment into your Sales Scorecard. Use the scorecard as a tool for all managers to align and measure their revenue generation and quota attainment.

Week Four

- The pillar management team holds its first integrated revenue meeting to discuss issues and determine revenue projects for the week. The group makes a presentation to the executive team.

- The CFO reviews calculations for ROI to help determine effectiveness.

Week Five

- The pillar management team meets with HR and the executive team to finalize job descriptions and responsibilities.

- The pillar management team generates a weekly executive report on group revenue issues and revenue quota met, and then submits a draft of the report to the executive committee for review.

Chapter 14
Integrated Pillar Management

- The executive committee and pillar management team meet to review all implementation issues and resolve any outstanding bottlenecks.

Week Six

- The pillar management team meets to generate another weekly executive report, and submits it to the executive committee.

- All job descriptions and quotas are finalized and become approved programs for the business development managers.

Implementation questions that need to be answered by management:

1. Will the pillar management team be part of the executive committee, report to it, or report to the vice president of sales?

2. How long will the transition time line be for the new compensation plan to take effect?

3. If the current sales forecasts are inaccurate and not based on a territory market potential capability, how will the executive committee assign a perceived fair quota to the business development management team?

Chapter 14
Integrated Pillar Management

4. What percentage of the total income of the pillar management should be based on quota attainment?

5. Who is the executive sponsor of this program—the vice president of sales, CEO, COO, or the team itself?

Use this Integrated Pillar Management program as a tool to integrate all departments to be responsible for revenue capture and your firm's revenue will grow proportionately to your team's commitment.

Sales management is complex. The faster your firm can integrate the whole company (or division) into a pillar management style program where all department heads work together as one synergistic group focused on revenue capture, the greater your success will be.

Chapter 15

Teaching Ethics and Morality

After reading this chapter, you will know:

- What three elements of ethical standards must be considered

- How to communicate and deploy ethical standards

Today more than ever, selling is not perceived to be a professional vocation by most people. Buyers who have had bad interactions with a real estate salesperson, an obnoxious telemarketer, or an unethical or immoral car salesperson perpetuate this belief.

Yet, the profession of sales is as old as mankind. People have always bartered or sold things of value to one another.

Your sales team is not you. They bring their own morals and business ethics to the job, based on their social and economic backgrounds, religious beliefs, and cultural upbringing. As a sales manager you must manage your sales team's actions because their actions are direct and indirect reflections of your company to your prospects.

Chapter 15
Teaching Ethics and Morality

Often, your salespeople will look to you for both formal and informal clues as to your sales ethics, and then they will feed off of that subliminal guidance.

If you have four-week sales quotas that you allow to become six-week quotas, contracts that are backdated, or allow unethical salespeople to operate with the rest of your sales team, you are sending out subliminal messages to your team that sales is more important than ethics.

Beyond this being an inappropriate philosophy, it is also bad business. Prospects generally do not start business relationships until the second sale. So, misrepresenting your business offering to get a quick sale, to win a sales contest, or to win a trip is not going to get you to the second sale.

Your sales team looks at sales management as a role model for expected behavior, so setting an ethical business standard is your job as much as the salesperson's individual responsibility.

You might wonder why I'm saying this. You are ethical. That may be true, but your sales team is your customer-facing brand, so it is critical that you communicate your ethical standards to your team members, so there is no second-guessing of what your expectations are.

Sales ethics goes beyond how your sales team interacts with existing customers and prospects. It

Chapter 15
Teaching Ethics and Morality

also includes how your sales team communicates with other sales team members and department staff.

There are three elements of ethical standards in sales that must be considered: (1) company standards, (2) building professional trust with the customer, and (3) individual responsibility. These elements are the responsibilities of both the management team and the salesperson.

6 Guidelines on How to Communicate and Deploy Ethical Standards to Your Sales Team

1. Ethics cannot be an implied sales process. It must be a verbalized and demonstrated process. You must communicate your expectations to your sales team on what type of sales action you expect and what you consider unacceptable. You must set the standards for all to be measured by. At least once a quarter, discuss sales morality, sales ethics, and internal company communication during a sales meeting.

2. Develop a detailed sign-off sheet to be used for product demonstrations with prospects or service descriptions provided to prospects, and have the prospects sign-off on the presentation or description, if possible.

Chapter 15
Teaching Ethics and Morality

3. Management must use a trickle-down ethical standards approach and demonstrate the same behavior they expect from the sales force. This includes not allowing 35-day months to happen during a sales contest, not accepting add-on sales freebies at the end of an agreement negotiation without authorization, or allowing salespeople to sell product and service capabilities that reside in the "gray area" that always seems to exist.

4. When hiring salespeople, make them sign (speak with your lawyer) an ethical business clause in their job description.

5. Communicate to your sales team on a monthly basis what is expected of them based on selling what you have—not what they want to sell.

Selling is an honorable and well-paid profession. But, like other professions, there are times when individuals stretch the truth to create income for themselves or visible achievement in front of others. When this happens, it is premeditated unethical behavior.

Sometimes, salespeople stretch the truth due to their over-enthusiasm during the sales cycle. From the buyer's point of view, this is still unethical behavior since the incorrect comments made by the salesperson may induce the prospect to buy . . . thus this behavior needs to be managed as well. Your job as a sales manager is to expect and receive ethical behavior from your sales team.

Chapter 15
Teaching Ethics and Morality

Conclusion

Sales Management Power Strategies explores multiple methodologies and best practices to help you and your firm develop and manage your sales team and the sales process. Some of these programs will take tremendous commitment and adaptation for your firm to implement and be successful.

Your firm's current position in its fiscal year and the executive sponsor for these different programs will affect the implementation time lines for any or all of these concepts.

Since some of these programs are culturally dramatic and will effect your entire organization, including budgeting, sales forecasting, job responsibilities, and compensation, none of the processes will be simple.

But, imagine that one year from today, you could have an integrated sales management program focused on individual and group production and managed on revenue capture. This program would reduce company politics, improve employee satisfaction, eliminate department silos, and create reachable sales forecasts. Simultaneously, it would make individual departments more focused on revenue ROI, reduce wasted expenses on unproductive programs, and help management understand the that revenue capture is a company responsibility.

Conclusion

So, the option becomes yours. Do you want to have a business structure that is not focused on revenue, but on department decentralization, or do you want to develop a centralized revenue capture program where the entire company is responsible to grow sales?

I wish you success and let me know how I can help.

Paul DiModica
DigitalHatch, Inc.
www.digitalhatch.com
Value Forward Sales and Marketing Advisors

Conclusion

Conclusion

Example Forms

The following pages contain forms you may want to use in building and managing your sales team

Current Sales Team Member Worksheet

List your salespeople based on their sales personality type.

Hunters:
1._____
2._____
3._____
4._____
5._____

Farmers:
1._____
2._____
3._____
4._____
5._____

Players:
1._____
2._____
3._____
4._____
5._____

Cowboys:
1._____
2._____
3._____
4._____
5._____

Politicians:
1._____
2._____
3._____
4._____
5._____

Half-Cycle Salespeople:
1._____
2._____
3._____
4._____
5._____

Trotters:
1._____
2._____
3._____
4._____
5._____

Non-Performers:
1._____
2._____
3._____
4._____
5._____

Candidate Primary Question Interview Sheet

Candidate's Name _____

Date Interviewed _____

Interviewer _____

Questions

1. How do you find prospects to sell?
   Cold Calling _____   Other _____

2. Did you hit your quota the last 2 years or more?
   Yes____   No____

3. What titles do you primarily sell to?
   Director/Above_____   Other _____

4. Did you make your quota by selling to new prospects?
   Yes____   No____

5. Have you been at your current job at least two years?
   Yes____   No____

6. Do you do your own executive demos/presentations?
   Yes____   No____

7. Have you personally invested in any sales training for yourself during the last year?
   Yes____   No____

8. Was at least 50% of your last W-2 from commissions?
   Yes____   No____

9. Would your current employer hire you again?
   Yes____   No____

10. Have you ever owned your own business?
    Yes____   No____

Ride-Along Form

Account Manager's Name_____

Ride-Along Date_____

Appointment Information

Account Name_____

Client Location_____

Appointment Time_____

Key Contacts to Meet:

Name_____Title_____

Name_____Title_____

Name_____Title_____

Name_____Title_____

Type of Meeting (Circle as many as needed):

Customer Service   New Prospect Opportunity   Existing Customer   Other

What product or service has the client bought or is interested in buying?
_____

Why will you win the business?
_____

Why will you lose the business?
_____

How do you create value for the prospect?
_____

As a sales manager, how should you respond during the meeting?
_____
_____

Weekly Sales Activities Report

Sales Rep Name: John Doe   **Week Ending:** May 31, 2006

Actions Completed Last Week

- Cold called 50 new prospects

- Had three on-site appointments with prospects

- Finished the Smith Proposal and hand delivered it

- Followed up on customer service issues with the Jones Company

Actions To Be Completed This Week

- Cold call 60 new prospects

- Meet with Smith again to negotiate proposal

- Two on-site meetings with prospects

- Mail direct sales letters to 100 prospects

Areas I Need Help In Or Management Involvement

- Currently need help with the ADL account on customer service issues

Sales Closing Audit

Today's date_____

Prospect/Client Name:_____

Contact Name:_____

Contact Title:_____

Person signing contract (if different from above):_____

Deal Value:_____

What are they buying?_____

Projected closing date:_____

What is their publicly stated budget?_____

Have you submitted your proposal yet? _____Yes _____No

Did you submit the proposal in person? _____Yes _____No

If no, how was proposal submitted? _____

Competitors in your deal_____

_____

_____

Last date of client contact:_____

Contact Method _____In-person _____Phone _____E-mail

Why will they buy?_____

Why will you lose?_____

Business consequence if they do not buy?_____

Next action step(s) _____By E-mail _____By phone _____In-person

_____

_____

Date of next action step_____

I need help from (circle all needed):

Operations   Sales Management   Senior Management   Service

Other   _____

Sales Team Monthly Skill Assessment

Account Manager's Name _____ Month _____

Cold Calling
Cold calls to new prospects .... _____
Cold calls to existing customers .... _____
Converting cold calls to appointments .... _____

Demos
Number of presentations per month .... _____
Number of webinars per month .... _____
Presentation conversion to proposals .... _____

Qualifying Prospects
Appointments with contract signer .... _____
Prospects have stated a budget .... _____
Prospects have stated an operational date .... _____
Prospects have stated a business pain or problem .... _____
Prospects have communicated your competition .... _____

Decision Influencer Management
Know why they will buy from you .... _____
Know why you will lose business .... _____
Identified who is influencing the contract signer .... _____
Know the political issues of the sale .... _____
Establish rapport with decision influencer .... _____
Understand how the decision is being made (RFP, etc.) .. _____
Has decision influencer verbalized your business value .. _____

Decision Maker/Contract Signer Management
Know why they will buy from you .... _____
Know why you will lose the business .... _____
Establish rapport with contract signer .... _____
Has decision maker verbalized your business value .... _____

Proposals
Proposals always approved by operations and/or accurate .... _____

Negotiation
Needs minimal help with deal negotiations .... _____
Closing ratio from proposal is 28% or better .... _____
Negotiation discount is within company guidelines .... _____

Sales Forecasting
Month-to-month sales forecast is at least 75% accurate .. _____
Sales forecasts are submitted timely .... _____

CRM/Contact Manager Maintenance
Enters data into CRM daily .... _____
CRM data is accurate and detailed .... _____

Expense Management
Expenses are submitted on time .... _____
Receipts are submitted with expense reports .... _____

Team Support
Works with team member positively _____

Index

Action Plans 147
Collectives................................. 199
Compensation Plans................. 117
Cultural Performance 104
Decline Stage............................. 63
Executive Management Types
    The CIO 23
    The Engineer 21
    The Entrepreneur 26
    The Family Run Business
        Executive.......................... 29
    The Hybrid 28
    The Inheritor 27
    The MBA............................... 24
    The Spin-Off/Corporate Person
        25
    The Wall Street Executive 30
Forecasting Moles..................... 173
Growth Stage.............................. 63
Incentive Program...................... 121
Innovative Stage 62
Interviewing
    Compatibility 92
    Dedication............................. 99
    Educational Investment 98
    Experience............................ 91
    Impression 90
    Income Verification 88
    Lead Generation Methods 96
    References 97
    Skill Sets............................... 93

Key Account Pursuit Team 70, 72
Lost Sales Analysis 162
Lost Sales Analysis Calculation.165
Market Research 169
Mature or plateau stage..............63
Meetings-Individual...................145
Meetings-Team.........................143
Quota Calculation 158
Revenue Capture Value Test 197
Ride-Along................................137
Role-Playing 129
Sales Activities Report..............149
Sales Closing Audit 185
Sales Cultural Audit Test 106
Sales Forecast..........................184
Sales Mentors..........................128
Sales Objections......................128
Sales Personality Types 52
    Cowboys...............................55
    Farmers................................53
    Half-Cycle Salespeople 57
    Hunters................................52
    Non-Performers....................58
    Players 54
    Politicians 56
    Trotters................................57
Sales Pipeline 184
Sales Process & Strategy Test....38
Sales Reports 128
Sales Scorecard 210
Virtual Offices 135

Other Services by Paul DiModica

Have Paul speak at your next event!
www.pauldimodica.com

Paul speaks worldwide on sales, marketing, strategy, and leadership delivering motivational and content-rich presentations that help audiences understand how to increase their personal and corporate performance based on proven strategic and tactical actions they can take immediately.

DigitalHatch Services
www.digitalhatch.com

Paul DiModica offers value forward sales and marketing services to clients seeking to increase corporate revenue including:

- Event Speaking
- Sales and Marketing Strategy Development and Consulting
- Executive Coaching
- Team Sales Training

Other Publications by Paul DiModica

Amazon.com Best Seller!

Value Forward Selling
How to Sell to Management
Become a peer in the boardroom, instead of a vendor waiting in the hallway
Available at www.digitalhatch.com

A sales training publication designed to help sales executives learn how to communicate their business value up front, successfully cold call and set up appointments with senior executives, give executive briefings where prospects will see them as a thought-leader, and negotiate deals from a non-commodity position. This book includes:

- **Proven sales techniques** that will help salespeople strategically sell complex offerings enabling you to increase your commissions and exceed your sales quotas
- **Accelerate sales cycles** with sales tactics that speed up the prospects' buying cycle to match the sales cycle
- **Discover how to map out** a sales cycle and target key accounts to focus on solution sales that generate the most revenue
- **The top five ways to sell** products or services quickly, efficiently and profitably, bypassing any business obstacles that stand in the way
- **Sales communication techniques** that position the salesperson as industry specialist
- **Proven cold calling techniques and scripts** make what is usually the most unpleasant part of sales a walk in the park

- **Generate senior management and C-level leads** with the four proven methods of lead generation that only work with "C-level" executives and senior management including using a proven "networking process" that creates inbound leads
- **How to find qualified buyers** instead of professional lookers
- Learn our demo and executive briefing model called the **"Three Box Monty"** that uses experiential sales techniques and business psychology to help prospects "experience" the value of the salesperson's product or service
- **How to use "Psychological ROI"** to get management prospects to buy from the salesperson instead of their competitors
- Learn the best sales methods to **manage competitors**
- Sales techniques that will help you close virtually every deal, every time.
- **Selling prospects on value, not price**, is the way to gain more clients. Now you can learn how to close the sale, even with a higher price.
- **Five specific steps you can take to develop a sales value proposition** for your product or service that will get your prospects to see you and your firm differently . . . immediately

Sign-up for Free Weekly Sales Strategy Newsletter *BDM News*
www.bdmnews.com

BDM News is the world's largest online magazine for sales and marketing executives in growth directed firms. Weekly get free tips on sales, strategy and marketing techniques to increase your sales success. *BDM News* is read in over 110 countries.

Printed in the United Kingdom
by Lightning Source UK Ltd.
124275UK00001B/57/A